susan SARANDON

actress-activist

susan SARANDON

MARC SHAPIRO
NEW YORK TIMES best-selling author of
J. K. ROWLING: THE WIZARD BEHIND HARRY POTTER

Prometheus Books
59 John Glenn Drive
Amherst, New York 14228-2197

Published 2001 by Prometheus Books

Inquiries should be addressed to
Prometheus Books
59 John Glenn Drive
Amherst, New York 14228–2197
VOICE: 716–691–0133, ext. 207
FAX: 716–564–2711
WWW.PROMETHEUSBOOKS.COM

05 04 03 02 01   5 4 3 2 1

Library of Congress Cataloging-in-Publication Data

Shapiro, Marc, 1949–
    Susan Sarandon : actress-activist / Marc Shapiro.
        p. cm.
    Includes index.
    ISBN 1–57392–928–X (alk. paper)
    1. Sarandon, Susan, 1946– 2. Motion picture actors and actresses—
United States—Biography. 3. Political activists—United States—Biography.
I. Title.

PN2287.S277 S53 2001
791.43'028'092—dc21
[B]   2001019991

Printed in the United States of America on acid-free paper

This book is dedicated to my wife, Nancy, and my daughter, Rachael, who fill the house with love and understanding. To my agent, Lori, for keeping the wolf away from the door. Thanks to Linda Regan for her guidance and encouragement. Assorted thanks to Bennie, Freda, Mike Kirby, Steve Ross, the gang at Poo Bah, Keri, Bad Baby, Chaos, and all the animals in the hood. Good film, good music, good art, and good books. And finally thanks to Susan Sarandon, who personifies the power of people to do great and mighty things.

PUBLISHER'S NOTE

This work draws heavily on Susan Sarandon's published interviews and public statements. All statements regarding Ms. Sarandon's state of mind or emotions are based either on actual statements by Ms. Sarandon or are based on reasonable inferences derived from these public sources. The author has made every effort to accurately portray Ms. Sarandon's life, career, and political passions, and the author hopes the reader will come to a greater understanding and respect for this remarkable woman through this work.

CONTENTS

UP THE ESTABLISHMENT

I t was a long, uneventful day . . . enlivened by Susan Sarandon.

The actress-activist was there with the morning coffee, all over the *New York Times* political pages. Giving life, meaning, and a real sense of excitement to the dark-horse presidential candidacy of Ralph Nader and his admittedly fringe Green Party. And no, hers was not the token lip service most celebrities prefer: Show up, mouth the platitudes, wait for the photo op, and then split. If the *Times* reporter got it correctly, Sarandon was speaking strictly from her heart and her belief. It was a sense of sincerity that those privy to her activism have come to know well: straightforward and self-effacing and taking great pains to make people forget that she is, in fact, somebody special. It was enough to make even this lifelong Democrat give Nader a second look.

Later that afternoon the talking head-gore fest that is the local Los Angeles news was interrupted by yet another political commercial. With the presidential election only a few weeks away, I was expecting mud slinging; long on bile and short on substance. But what I got was Susan Sarandon, calmly exhorting viewers to donate their cell phones to a battered-women's clinic. It was easily the obscurest of causes I had heard about yet. However, Sarandon's sincerity and the expressive, determined look in her eyes and conviction in her voice could not be denied. If there was a cell phone handy, it was hers.

Finally, staring halfheartedly at two sub-500 teams slugging it out on ESPN, the phone rings. My wife picks it up, says it's Susan Sarandon, and hands me the phone. It is indeed Sarandon, by way of a computerized recording, insisting that if I wanted the particulars of Ralph Nader's economic plan, hit the pound sign. Honestly, my interest in Ralph Nader at this point goes only as far as his ability to stick it to the Democrats and the Republicans. But Sarandon made it all seem so urgent, so important that the candidates' numbers game be heard that I hit pound and listened until my eyes glazed over.

Susan Sarandon made me read, listen, and, for a little while, believe in the power of a vocal minority to bring about change.

It is the rare celebrity who has exhibited the ongoing sense of political and social outrage that has seen Susan Sarandon manning the literal and figurative barricades since the early eighties. Jane Fonda, of whom Sarandon can be considered a logical-philosophical descendant, had it before she went soft and married into corporate America. Martin Sheen has it. So does Richard Dreyfuss.

But at the end of the day, there are not many who can be counted on regularly to fight the good fight.

Sarandon, in a style hauntingly reminiscent of the sixties, brandishes a walk-the-walk attitude that is brash in its worldview and compelling in its earnestness. Sarandon does her homework. No statement leaves her mouth without her having the facts and research to back it up. She is not big on photo ops and the only time you will find her at a soup kitchen or a homeless shelter is when the cameras are not around. And she is not one of your basic checkbook liberals. She will contribute financially but then, in the same motion, link arms and march on city hall. All of which goes a long way toward explaining why Sarandon made the Top 40 on both the FBI and CIA hit list. She's been cuffed and arrested. Rebel! Rebel! What's not to like?

Sarandon has not let life in a fishbowl compromise her beliefs. Her long-standing, live-in relationship with the younger actor Tim Robbins laughs defiantly in the face of social taboo. She has often risked the ire of traditional Hollywood with her outspoken ways. No pulpit is sacred—especially the platform that was the 1992 Academy Awards where she exhorted a roomful of top producers, directors, and stars to think with their hearts rather than their egos.

Oh, and did I forget to mention that Susan Sarandon is also one hell of an actress? Loved her in *Bull Durham* with that weary, over-the-top sexuality. Marveled at the power and quiet intensity she brought to her role in *Thelma & Louise*. *Dead Man Walking*? *Atlantic City*? The hot eroticism of *The Hunger*? And, as young, virginal ingenues go, her Janet Weiss in the outrageous *The Rocky Horror Picture Show* is one for the ages. Pushing the envelope and totally deconstructing expectations? Take a look at *Light Sleeper*. Need an exercise in controlled subtlety? I'm sure you can dig up a copy of *Pretty Baby*. And lest we forget: there's *Joe* with Sarandon in a quintessential drug-induced haze.

She has been able to walk the tightrope of renaissance woman, with her causes and hit movies a result of them. Yet she has made it to the other side, a true cause for celebration. How she came to hold her profession and her activism so dear is an object lesson we could all stand to learn.

Susan Sarandon is worth two books: one that celebrates her skills as an actress; another that celebrates her activism and her humanity. This book celebrates her complete world, a world that is constantly changing.

I haven't heard from Susan Sarandon in a few days now. But the presidential election is only six days away.

So I'm sure I will.

Marc Shapiro

"WE ARE PISSED OFF! HAPPY MOTHER'S DAY!"

Y ou know you're in trouble when your lover tries to stereotype you.

That was Susan Sarandon's predicament in 1999 when Tim Robbins, her live-in lover for more than a decade and the father of her two sons, was discussing a role he wanted her to play in his 1930s look at U.S. censorship and the entertainment industry, *Cradle Will Rock*. Hallie Flanagan was a two-fisted crusader for government funding for the arts. Robbins argued, passionately and quite logically, that Sarandon would be perfect for the part. Sarandon trusted her life partner's instincts and, in her heart of hearts, knew he was right.

And for Sarandon, that was the problem.

Hallie was, in many ways, too much like the crusading nun she had played in her Oscar-winning turn in *Dead Man Walking*. Too much like the advocate for racial equality in *A Dry White Season* and too much like the waitress turned angry, gun-toting Establishment fighter in the wildly controversial *Thelma & Louise*. She was not too far removed from the template that had marked her greatest moments as an actress. For Sarandon the idea, at this juncture, of openly embracing safe creative ground did not compute.

The actress, as was her style, wanted to shake things up and public perception be damned. And so she lobbied for and ultimately convinced Robbins that she would be perfect for the part of Italian propagandist Margherita Sarfatti, who vamped around this fictional world in sexy thirties fashions and "fuck-me pumps."

"I told Tim that people didn't have to pay $10 to see me harassing Congress," she told a *Calgary Sun* reporter. "They could just turn on their TVs."

Sarandon's joke was not lost on Robbins—nor on anybody with a remote inkling as to what Susan Sarandon is about. Because in the life of Susan Sarandon, there has already been a lot to see.

In March of that year, Sarandon, linked arm in arm with local New York activists Floyd Flake and Al Sharpton, joined protesters with the Center for Constitutional Rights as they marched on New York's 1 Police Plaza to protest the killing of unarmed street vendor Amadou Diallo, who was "accidentally" shot forty-one times by four New York police officers. These were tense times on the streets of New York. The police force had long been suspect, especially in the racial profiling and preconceived stereotypes that marked its dealings with minorities. Charges of police brutality were occurring on an almost daily basis. But the seemingly unprovoked shooting of Diallo had lit the fuse on already explosive tensions.

"We Are Pissed Off! Happy Mother's Day!"

At one point in the loud but peaceful demonstration, the police ruled it an unlawful assembly and began making arrests. The assembled media aimed their cameras at those who were about to symbolically defy authority and be led away in cuffs. And a good many of them were pointed in the direction of Sarandon. The actress had gone this route before but, admittedly, did not relish having her children see her being lead away in handcuffs on the six o'clock news. Not many would have blamed her if she had discreetly slipped away from the crowd. But that was not her way. She was not playing games.

Sarandon sat down on the pavement and went limp as the police waded into the crowd and began making arrests. Sarandon was handcuffed. As she was led away, she yelled out to nearby reporters that an injustice had led to this demonstration. She was taken to New York's central jail in a police van packed tight with demonstrators and ended up spending seven hours in a jail cell before being released. But she had a souvenir to take back to her children who were always well aware of their mother's political activities and the possibility that she might be arrested—the plastic handcuffs that had been wrapped around her wrists.

In October of 1999, Sarandon, once again outraged, took to the battlements outside the Brooklyn Museum to join others in protesting Mayor Rudy Giuliani's attempts to block a controversial art exhibit, "Sensations," from being shown and cutting funds to the museum in a thinly disguised attempt to get them evicted. For Sarandon, this

17

was returning to her activist roots for, in the mid-1980s as a member of the fledgling Creative Coalition, Sarandon had faced down Congress in its own backyard with a succinct yet passionate speech that was integral in blocking conservative elements from putting the clamps on funding for the National Endowment for the Arts.

On this day, in front of one thousand people, Sarandon evoked quiet but strong sentiments couched in the First Amendment. A couple of months after she had given her speech, Mayor Giuliani pulled back on his threats and extended the funding for the museum. Hers and the other voices that criticized the mayor were rewarded with a victory.

This Susan Sarandon, who stood up for her beliefs, is the one that most of us are familiar with. But there is the less publicized side to her as well.

A month later, Sarandon, away from the cameras and with nary a hint of media attention, braved a frigid New York afternoon to help a local food bank for the homeless called City Harvest by helping pick up food at supermarkets and driving over to a Bowery soup kitchen where she joined in the distribution of the food to those in need. Those connected to City Harvest acknowledged her presence and ignored her celebrity—which was exactly the way she wanted it.

While Sarandon was surely aware of her celebrity and its power to do good works, she craved those moments when she could dress down and interact with people on a real-world level. At this level, she reasoned, the causes were the real stars and she was just another fan trying to be helpful. It kept her grounded in a way that few celebrities would ever begin to fathom.

This quiet act was inevitably followed by more vociferous ones. On Mother's Day, Sarandon took part in a Washington, D.C., antigun rally where she began an alternately fiery and enlightened speech by saying, "We are pissed off! Happy Mother's Day!" A rally against the encroachment of corporate monopolies, once again in Washington, D.C., also saw the actress in its ranks.

Her participation in these high-profile demonstrations was typical of Sarandon's methodical approach to activism. Although sympathetic to both causes, she had not been quick to be a public voice. She studied their positions, absorbed the statistics, and, once she felt well informed about both sides of the issue, then and only then did she decide to make her voice heard.

And, when it comes to causes she believes in, Sarandon has not been one to avoid biting the hand that literally feeds her. She was a firebrand at a number of protests against Paramount Studios when its television wing trotted out a syndicated television talk show by the notorious antigay radio psychologist Laura Schlessinger. A statement made during one of those demonstrations was vintage Sarandon, cutting in its subtlety and its impact.

"Laura Schlessinger is clearly in dire need of compassion, education, and a good shrink herself."

In April 1989 Sarandon appeared at a Washington, D.C., abortion rights march while extremely pregnant with her second child. Detractors might unreasonably construe protesting while in her condition as the height of hypocrisy and mockery. But Sarandon's appearance more than pointed up the fact that she was there to support a woman's right to choose, to make her own decision whether or not to have a baby.

Sarandon's activist choices have not always run to safe, liberal causes. She has long been an ardent supporter of the extremely militant gay group Act Up and once appeared on the *Today* show to promote a movie with an Act Up button prominently displayed.

Beginning in 1983, and at a time when the prevailing U.S. attitude in Central America was hawkish but not necessarily on the morally defensible side, Sarandon made Nicaragua a cause célèbre, despite rumbles from her agents and close friends that her taking on "conservative" government and, by association, traditional Hollywood attitudes might stifle her career.

Sarandon ignored those warnings and continues to heed no such advice whenever she decides to take a stand. Because, truth be known, Susan Sarandon loves a good fight, when she feels she is in the right.

Flood relief, endangered wildlife, constitutional rights, Meals on Wheels. The list could go on ad infinitum. Suffice it to say, Susan Sarandon is an activist and not just the token Hollywood variety: big on charity lunches, sound bites on the six o'clock news, and the Radical Chic label.

In fact, more than one interview with Sarandon has been conducted in the midst of her doing good works. When she is not on a film set or tending to the needs of

her three children and longtime live-in lover and companion, Tim Robbins, the actress-activist can most likely
be found handing out food to the homeless, packing up
supplies for hurricane victims, or speaking at rallies for
nontraditional political candidates and causes.

Make no mistake, Sarandon does like her quiet time and
often takes great pains to insure it for herself and her family.
She will rarely work outside of New York when her children
are in school. It is a hard and fast rule that cost her a part
in a movie she really wanted to do in 1996, the Jane Cam-
pion film *Portrait of a Lady*. But it has been the rare time
that the actress has been too tired or too busy to not put in
even a token appearance on behalf of a worthy cause.

Sarandon comes to her involvement in a myriad of
political and social causes with a real-world, questioning
attitude that easily eschews image and celebrity with a
sense of old-world honesty and a simple striving for truth
and justice. She can be explosive in this arena; a naturally
educated and determined firebrand. Hers is a gut-check
kind of activism—one that comes from her heart.

She was the only woman present at an AIDS informa-
tional meeting in the early eighties, long before the cause
caught the attention of Elizabeth Taylor and the rest of the
Hollywood red ribbon crowd. When the Persian Gulf War
became the new "good war," Sarandon was one of the few
to say the emperor, in the guise of the U.S. government and
a renewed hawkish environment, was wearing no clothes.

The causes do not have to be high profile to get her
attention; in fact, Sarandon's feeling has always been the

more grass roots the better when it comes to her involvement. Which is why she has actively lobbied on behalf of We Can, a New York-based bottle-and-can redemption center for the homeless and the Rosenberg Fund for Children, which offers financial support for children whose parents have been targeted by politicians and conservative political groups for their progressive activities.

Sarandon does not see herself as the token celebrity in her good works but rather a conduit, bringing to the public what she considers crucial information about important organizations. "By doing so, I ask the questions they [the public] want to know and I help them to better understand the issues," she explained in a *Variety* interview. "That's how I see my role."

Her role in the activist world has not been easy. Celebrity did not automatically grant her entry into the halls of protest. Many involved in real-world issues have often looked askance at celebrities who only seem to be in it for the publicity and the tax write-off. If Sarandon had been anything less than sincere, she would have been spotted immediately and, figuratively, shown the door.

In that sense Sarandon was fortunate. When she found activism in the early eighties, she was little more than a working actress with little stock in celebrity. Which was why she was able to move effortlessly between the worlds of fantasy and reality.

And why she has her supporters.

Kathy Engel, the head of MADRE, a U.S.-based organization that brings aid and comfort to Nicaraguan families, has said, "There's nothing dilletantish about the way she decides to engage in the world. If she wasn't deeply committed she wouldn't take the risks that she does."

Geena Davis became a Sarandon fan during the making of *Thelma & Louise* when she went to bat for Davis when director Ridley Scott insisted that Davis do a nude scene. "She's my role model. She's crazy, strong, and outspoken. A real troublemaker."

"She understands her place in the universe," said longtime friend Anna Gross. "She walks down the street as herself."

Lynn Cohen, Sarandon's friend for over twenty years, once summed up the actress by saying, "You don't feel jealous of her. She's not this competitive bitch."

Given her wide range of interests, it should come as no surprise that her politics are hard to classify. She admits to being a card-carrying member of the ACLU but she has never seen herself as a radical lefty. In fact, the only thing predictable about Susan Sarandon's politics is their unpredictability. Hers is a personal hybrid of ideals, and being forthright in their defense has often come at a price.

She was once accosted on the street while walking with her young child in her arms and called a "Communist cunt." When she took an unpopular stand on the U.S. involvement in the Gulf War, Sarandon drew the ire of both the FBI and the CIA. Her pro-Haiti outburst as a presenter at the 1992 Academy Awards earned her an unofficial blacklisting by the Hollywood Academy committee that lasted a year. Hate mail? She's had her share and then some.

Sarandon has often admitted that being in the forefront of unpopular or misunderstood causes has taken its toll and that it can be a lonely existence.

"Whenever you're trying to change the status quo, by definition you're going to be inappropriate," she told the *Hollywood Reporter*. "But I have no regrets."

Susan Sarandon talks and we listen. Why?

Because she is not hypocritical. She does not drop a dime for gun control and then do a gratuitous action film. She has not been one to play the Hollywood game. When her experiences in the films *Tempest*, *The Witches of Eastwick*, and *White Palace* were less than stellar, Sarandon was quick to break one of the biz's big taboos and bad-mouthed those films' shortcomings to the press.

She knows crap when she sees it and while the actress has admittedly done more than her share of fluff and the rare piece of out and out garbage, she has made it plain that she knew exactly what she was doing and that there was a reason for it. When she willingly agreed to participate in an admittedly soft script entitled *Compromising Positions*, she freely acknowledged that she was doing the film for solely mercenary reasons: the money would pay for the necessities of her soon-to-be-born first child.

Her candor has often put her on the wrong side of Hollywood and, in subtle and not too subtle ways, has slowed her career. Long after the point where she was considered at the top of her game, Sarandon was still having to audition for roles. She has, often by choice, not made the kind of money afforded actresses in the upper echelon of Hollywood. In fact, well into her forties, Hollywood had regulated her to a perennial third or fourth choice in the pecking order; somebody they would call on when the big stars were too busy, too expensive, or not interested.

Sarandon has freely admitted that she has often sabotaged her own career. Taking an average of eighteen months off after the birth of each of her children regularly set her back. Sarandon, on that subject, has often jokingly said that she has been discovered three or four times by Hollywood.

But Susan Sarandon's professional life has ultimately thrived and is marked by the same integrity that marks her private crusades. Her career has been marked by box-office smashes (*The Witches of Eastwick*, *The Client*, *Bull Durham*), cult hits (*The Rocky Horror Picture Show*, *The Hunger*, *Joe*), and art house-independent works (*Illuminata*, *Bob Roberts*). But, inevitably, Sarandon has been drawn to films that reflect a political or social concern; even if only on the periphery.

And it has been in those cases that Hollywood has served her well: *Dead Man Walking* with its death-penalty theme; *Thelma & Louise*, a blatantly feminist tale done up as a modern-day western; *Lorenzo's Oil* with its not-too-veiled parallel to the current AIDS crisis; *A Dry White Season* with antiapartheid on its thematic mind; and even *White Palace* with its romance between an older woman and a younger man that pushes the social envelope.

Sarandon has insisted on more than one occasion that it is the strength of the role and not necessarily the political nature of the script that has drawn her to a work; her criteria being characters that have an element of truth to them and stories that deal decidedly with the real world. Consequently Sarandon does not, by normal Hollywood standards, work very much, which is fine by her because she says it would take only an exceptional film to pry her away from her family.

Sarandon has always made a point of stating that her film career has never been colored by her political and social attitude and that she has never deliberately looked to play socially conscious activist roles. Her formula for picking roles has been relatively simple: a character with dignity who goes on an odyssey of change and that occasionally surprises with unexpected actions and emotions.

Louis Malle, who directed the actress in the films *Pretty Baby* and *Atlantic City* and who admittedly had both a personal and professional interest in Sarandon, once proclaimed, "She is regarded by fellow professionals as one of the very best actresses of her generation."

Joel Schumacher, who directed Sarandon in *The Client*, has said, "She is a big star. Many actors who have had much hotter launches than Susan didn't last as long as she has. Which tells you something about how smart she is."

Tim Robbins, who has directed her in the films *Dead Man Walking* and *Cradle Will Rock*, knows there is a certain amount of bias in any assessment he makes of Sarandon.

"But she's a great actress," he told the *Australian Herald Sun*. "You know one of the things I love about her? She really has got balls. She has the guts to do different things. As an actress she has the courage to be unsympathetic, and there are few people who do that."

Unexpected has been very much the watchword in

Susan Sarandon's life. She has metamorphosed from a good Catholic girl, steeped in traditional values, into someone who has raced to embrace the unorthodox in her personal life. Following a failed marriage to actor Chris Sarandon (with whom she had previously lived for three years), the actress engaged in a very public affair with director-writer Franco Amurri that produced a daughter. Sarandon, much earlier in her career, would have another public relationship with director Louis Malle. Since 1988, she has been living with actor Tim Robbins and the union has produced two children.

But ask her about the possibility of marriage and she will blithely toss it aside with a roll of her wide, expressive eyes. Sarandon honestly feels that she is not deliberately flying in the face of prevailing social mores but is just living her life according to her own set of personal values and rules.

"I believe in love and trust and commitment but not in marriage," she said in a candid interview with *Cosmopolitan*. "Marriage may do something for lawyers and mothers but not for husbands and wives."

Susan Sarandon arrives in the year 2001 in a state of grace. Her career flourishes and her activism remains above reproach. However the actress is self-effacing in the honors and plaudits that have been placed at her feet. Quite simply she sees herself as an ordinary person who happens to be in an extraordinary position.

And at the end of the day, she considers herself quite lucky.

"I'm always incredibly shocked that I still have a

career," she once explained to the *London Independent*. "I've done everything wrong so there must be some kind of angel watching over me."

chapter two

"I WAS A SPACEY CHILD"

S usan Sarandon once said that her parents "both had very strange childhoods."

In hindsight her comment was rather conservative. The reality was that the early lives of Phillip Leslie Tomalin and Lenora Marie Criscione were emotionally scarred experiences, irreparably marred by the lack of a normal family upbringing.

Phillip's father died when the child was quite young and he was subsequently shuttled off to live with his older brother. Raised within a nontraditional family unit and subject to no true parental authority, Phillip scraped through his high school years emotionally scattered and with a sense of rootlessness that later translated into the equally nomadic life of a nightclub singer and a stint in the military during World War II. One day, on one of the endless train rides to another job, he ran into an attractive young woman named Lenora Criscione who had her own story to tell.

Lenora's mother grew up in an America that was in between wars and in economic decline. Outwardly a normal child full of childhood notions and good cheer, inwardly the child struggled with emotional ailments and insecurities that would trouble her throughout her life. Her mother grew into young womanhood, and met and married Lenora's father in a civil ceremony in Setauket, Long Island, in 1920. Shortly after their marriage, Lenora's mother became pregnant.

Lenora's birth was a time of joy for the Criscione family. But the joy would be short-lived. Lenora's mother did her best to be a good wife and mother but suffered from an increasing inability to cope with everyday chores and responsibilities. The Criscione marriage was clearly in jeopardy. By the time Lenora turned three, her mother's mental and emotional torment had gotten to be too much and she walked out on her husband and daughter. Lenora's parents would subsequently divorce.

Lenora's father did his best to hold the family together but the young child did not fare well at the sudden loss of her mother. Lenora was placed in a Catholic girls' school where she would spend her childhood surrounded by the often-restrictive dictum of the church and all too clearly defined prejudices against the child who had been abandoned by her mother. It was little wonder that Lenora spent much of her early life as a quiet, withdrawn child who made friends with great difficulty and was often counseled for her lack of direction. And so it was a very young, inexperienced Lenora who was attempting to find her way in the outside world for the first time as a college student when she met Phillip.

The couple found they had a lot in common, particularly as it pertained to their respective childhoods. Their Welsh-Italian backgrounds were the ideal complement to their already deeply ingrained conservative values. And, truth be known, what formed an immediate, strong bond between the couple was that they both needed love and some semblance of normalcy in their lives. After a relatively short courtship, the couple married.

Clearly they played by the conventions of the times. Courtships were never very long in the 1940s and 1950s. There was never a whole lot of time to really get to know a potential life partner. So Phillip and Lenora prepared to settle down and raise a family.

Feeling the need to be the constant in his family's life that had been absent in his, Phillip gave up the itinerant life of a nightclub singer and settled into the more sedate occupation of advertising salesman. In later years, he would move into television production and pilot the fortunes of Milton Berle in the golden age of television.

The couple settled in the Jackson Heights section of Queens in New York. By all accounts they led a comfortable, if somewhat insulated existence. Lenora was quite happy to be the stay-at-home housewife and the couple rarely saw the need to venture out and deal with the world outside. They appeared to have few if any friends and did not socialize outside of an immediate circle of relatives.

Lenora became pregnant not too long after the couple married. This was a happy, exciting time for Phillip and Lenora. Although far from being demonstrative, you could see it in their broad smiles and hear it in their excited tones as they talked about names. Picking out furniture for the baby's room was a major, joyous undertaking.

On October 4, 1946, Susan Abigail Tomalin was born. She would not be an only child.

Being strict Catholics, and perhaps looking to compensate for the lonely childhoods they experienced, Phillip and Lenora had long ago decided on a big family and, three years later, the second of what would ultimately be a total of nine Tomalin children was on its way. But as the family grew, the ability to financially afford to live in Jackson Heights became unfeasible and so the family packed up and moved across the river to the more affordable New Jersey suburb of Metuchen.

Being the first child, Sarandon had a lot of attention lavished on her by her parents. Sarandon grew up a bright, perceptive, introverted, and ultimately contrary girl who instinctively, through such childhood activities as rotating the dresses on all her dolls, was already striving to make things fair and equitable in her world. That she was compulsive, introspective, and not quite in sync with her immediate world and with her parents' notion of the way things should be, was a given in her very young mind. But it seemed a quite natural way for the young Susan to behave. If she was doing anything wrong, her mind could not comprehend it.

It must have also been a constant source of consternation on her parents' part when they discovered that their first child had a mind of her own. But, as they would quickly discover, Sarandon was already well on the way to developing some psychological quirks of her own.

"I was a very spacey child," she has confessed. "I was always someplace else. If you look at home movies of us as kids, you see everyone else together doing something normal, while I'm off in the corner, just staring at something."

And as more and more children increased the household, Sarandon became increasingly combative and distant from her younger siblings. She often recalled the sense of a wall between herself and the other Tomalin children and, since the next oldest child was three years her junior, Sarandon often felt like a surrogate parent which, she recalled, made her feel even more isolated.

Sarandon's isolation was due in large part to the sheer numbers of her family. And admittedly nine children were a handful that could easily lead to chaos and confusion.

By all accounts, Sarandon's relationship with her siblings did improve as they got older. While it was never overtly stated, it was Sarandon's opinion that she was always being held up as an example, both good and bad, to the younger children by her parents. In later years, Sarandon's siblings reportedly would echo those sentiments but acknowledged that they felt they had grown up a closely knit family and that everybody, childhood squabbles notwithstanding, got along.

It was to their credit that Phillip and Lenora, while often puzzled at Susan's seemingly strange introverted nature, did not take great pains to direct her in a different direction. Whether it was their own childhoods, and their own lack of parental guidance, or a feeling that she would eventually outgrow her uncompromising nature, Susan's parents seemed content to let her go her own way.

As the family grew, Sarandon found herself saddled with much of the responsibility for her younger siblings, making sure her younger brothers and sisters got their meals and dressed warmly. These were chores she willingly did. "It grounded me," she said in an *US* magazine interview. "Whatever measure of common sense I now have came as a result of being the oldest of the brood."

Contrary to many celebrity childhoods, Sarandon's introverted nature did not translate into a desire to act. There was a flirtation with the idea of being a dancer that stemmed from her early coordination and ease of movement. But that idea was ultimately shelved. If anything, Susan was, in those early years, not particularly drawn to any idea of what she wanted to be and seemed to very much live in the moment.

There was a natural sense of curiosity in the young girl that, as she would later recall, often put her in direct emotional conflict with her parents and their insulated, nonpolitical household. Conversations around the ever-crowded dinner table were limited to the most mundane things such as her father's day at work, how the kids were doing at school, and what had gone on in the household. Spirited discussions were nearly nonexistent. Politics were never discussed. That people were suffering social injustices outside their four walls was of no interest to Phillip and Lenora.

"It wasn't a house where we knew anything was going on outside," Sarandon once explained to *Mother Jones* magazine. In later years she would concede that she grew up with an overwhelming sense of ignorance and isolation about the world around her. And it was a state that she would soon begin to resent and finally rebel against.

Susan entered a Roman Catholic elementary school in 1951. The school was essentially a continuation of her home life. Her classmates, like her, came from large families, and were raised according to a conservative, rigid interpretation of their life, religion, and surroundings. There were no black students and any mention of Jews in the school's curriculum was always couched in less than positive terms. This was not an education designed to do anything more than turn out passive, nonquestioning children.

Against this confining environment, Sarandon stood out. The young girl had quite naturally cultivated a serious albeit childish sense of rebelliousness that immediately put her in conflict with the school's nuns. She was not willing to take anything they said as the final word and was always quick with a question.

"I was asking all the wrong questions even back in the third grade," she recalled in a 1995 *Buzz* magazine interview. "When the nuns explained how you had to be married in the Catholic Church or you weren't married, I asked, 'Well, how could Joseph and Mary be married, since Jesus didn't come up with it until later?' They sent me out to stand in the hall. I was told I had an overabundance of original sin."

These incidents inevitably got back to Phillip and Lenora, which, even at her early age, began to strain the relationship between parents and child. The other Tomalin children were, relatively speaking, toeing the traditional line set down by their parents and so, in oh so subtle ways, Sarandon was already being cast as the unorthodox child.

Conversations regarding conduct usually started out softly in the Tomalin household. But Sarandon's insistence on asking what her parents considered out-of-bounds questions and insisting on an answer would eventually rile her normally soft-spoken parents. They could not send her out in the hall but Sarandon would often end up being sent to her room.

Sarandon would often be, by degrees, amused and shocked at those moments when her overriding curiosity would result in anger and frustration on the part of her parents. Because the reality was that Sarandon was trying real hard to be the perfect girl and could not fathom how her actions were getting on everybody's nerves.

And there was much in her demeanor that justified her growing reputation as an outsider. Sarandon had always been an introverted child, inclined toward compulsive behavior such as rehearsing all summer with neighborhood kids on plays that they would never put on. But Susan, as she made her way through the Catholic school system, was already beginning to look outward.

She had too many questions and not enough satisfactory answers. She was looking more and more upon religion as an unpleasant chore. Even as a preteen, Sarandon sensed that there was a lot that she was missing out on in life. And she was determined to catch up.

Following her graduation from elementary school, it was a given that Sarandon would follow in the Tomalin family tradition and attend the local Catholic secondary institutions. But Susan insisted that she wanted to attend a public junior high school and after much arguing, and the ever-widening gap between mother and daughter, Sarandon was reluctantly allowed to enroll in a public junior high school in nearby Edison, New Jersey.

In hindsight, Sarandon felt she had put up a persuasive argument but there was a lot in her parents' demeanor that indicated they felt the best way to deal with their eldest daughter at that point was to, figuratively, throw up their hands and let her do what she wanted. Although still largely an all-white suburb of New Jersey, Edison was a lot less cloistered, by degrees more working class in its collective thinking and more liberal than Metuchen.

Life in public school was an eye-opening experience for Sarandon.

"It was a great education to actually meet Jewish people who weren't ashamed of being Jewish," she related in a *Rolling Stone* interview. "And I had boys in my class."

Sarandon's years in public junior high and high school began a slow but steady climb out of her restrictive upbringing. While she was far from being a lapsed Catholic, Sarandon was finding a new kind of stimulation in her daily interaction with her classmates and more liberal-minded teachers to fuel her growing enthusiasm for the bigger picture that lay before her. Despite her parents' concerns that public school would corrupt her morals and turn her into a wild child, Sarandon was far from a problem teen.

She did not have a steady boyfriend, although she did attend the junior prom with a boy her mother approved of. There is nothing in the public record, or that Sarandon is willing to admit, that leads to the notion that she was sexually active (in fact she would remain a virgin until she met her future husband) or involved in drinking and other temptations that were coming into vogue in the late fifties and early sixties. But she did go through some obvious changes, although she would not blossom into full-blown rebellion until her college years.

What her parents and even her younger siblings had considered a phase manifested itself in Sarandon adopting the then-rebellious uniform of pierced ears, high boots, and hair which had grown to the young girl's waist. Many a night, Sarandon would come home looking every bit the rebel and would be ignored by her family.

That Sarandon and her siblings were often left to go through both big and small moments in their lives without much input or stroking from their parents was the true, unspoken tragedy in the Tomalin household. The reality was that the consequence of having so many children was that Lenora was always involved in the needs of the infants and had little time for the children who were old enough to fend for themselves. And after a hard day's work, Phillip could be counted on for little more than polite dinner-table conversation.

Being the oldest, Sarandon soon became aware of the lack of that all-important missing emotional connection between children and parents, despite the fact that she would often state that there was much more to the Tomalin family dynamic.

"My parents had no chance in hell of having a good time with us," she said in *More*. "There were just too many kids."

There were increasingly bitter arguments in which her mother would blindly lash out and accuse Sarandon of being immoral. While he was a bit more approachable than her mother, she would often paint a picture of her father as equal parts loving, eccentric, and difficult. Sarandon has long remained silent on the topic of her relationship with her parents and has often wavered on what, to her, was a touchy subject and often, no doubt, subject to selective denial.

An interview with *Redbook* in the early nineties took an abrupt turn from pleasant to uptight and defensive when the question was asked what gifts she felt she received from her parents. She replied, "There is absolutely no evidence of my parents in terms of my development."

The underlying resentment toward her parents continued in recent years as she has conceded that hers was, in fact, not a happy childhood. "Which may have something to do with my ending up as an actress."

SUSAN SARANDON

The relationship between Phillip and Lenora had also begun to disintegrate under the pressure of years of pent-up emotions and unhappiness. Sarandon had always sensed a decided difference in temperament between her parents and sensed, as by now an emotionally receptive teen, that they were not happy together. Phillip and Lenora would divorce shortly after Sarandon left home.

Sarandon graduated from high school in 1964. Essentially at a loss about what to do with her life, the young woman decided to go to college "because that's what you did in the sixties." The idea of continued formal education did not really appeal to her. But, at that point, neither did settling into a bland, dead-end job. She chose Catholic University in Washington, D.C., the reason being that she could live off campus with her grandparents.

"My sole ambition was to get out of Jersey," she remembered in *Elle*. "Once I did that I thought my life would just unfold."

The year Sarandon started Catholic University was a pivotal one in the political and social evolution of the United States. Camelot had crumbled with an assassin's bullet. Socially the country was in a state of flux. There was talk of free love and equal rights for women. Civil rights and the march of the Beats toward a more utopian lifestyle was in the air. Hippies proliferated and Dylan spoke of steady winds of change. Sarandon, in those early freshman days, was more interested in finding a viable major and getting her classes than expressing her political and social outrage.

Sarandon, much like her parents had been, was basically cast adrift in academic life without a direction. In the purest sense of the word, Sarandon did not know what she wanted to do with her life at a time when the popular credo was "Do your own thing." Instead she spent a lot of time going through the motions in those early days of higher learning and not really accomplishing much.

Despite the fact that "I had never wanted to be an actor" Sarandon decided on a drama major with an emphasis on English classes and a chosen minor of philosophy. It was, for the time, a typical slapdash menu of liberal arts classes, including, oddly enough, a course in military science, designed to mark time until a viable major, a stable job, or something else turned up. Not that the wide-reaching nature of her courses was of overriding concern for, as she readily admitted in a *Parade* magazine interview, "I never studied."

But she was not idle. While Sarandon continued to insist that she did not have the slightest interest in acting as a profession (and as an underclassman she was not allowed to act in major plays), she did find the atmosphere and the people in the drama department stimulating and felt that for a novice with little interest, she could hold her own in readings and informal freshman performances with a raw, albeit quiet, sense of expressiveness. Her teachers and fellow classmates instinctively felt that Sarandon might have just what it takes to be an actress if she applied herself in that direction. But when approached with those compliments, she would invariably toss them aside because she was really not that interested. In fact, during those early days at Catholic University, she had few goals outside of possibly teaching.

When not toying with the idea of higher education as a vocation, Sarandon worked at a number of jobs: cleaning apartments, working the switchboard at the drama department, and, with her striking looks and skinny frame, landing the occasional modeling assignment. Of the latter, it is no small irony that her most high-profile job at the time was to pose in front of the newly completed Watergate Hotel for a brochure.

And it was in this arena that, with baby steps, the young woman began to find a sense of self. While growing up, Sarandon had never thought of herself as being beautiful. In fact, when it had been called to her attention by her high school classmates that her eyes were too big, she began to squint. But in those modeling assignments, Sarandon began to see that there was, indeed, a nice, slightly exotic in an Egyptian sort of way, look to her. Instinctively, she felt comfortable in front of the camera although, intellectually, she did not see rhyme or reason to what she was doing.

But, like her approach to her studies, Sarandon was not approaching work with much direction or passion. She once told *Playboy*, "I did some modeling in those days, not because I wanted to be a model but because it was a good way to pay off debts."

Despite an outwardly confident appearance, Sarandon was still carrying around much of her childhood baggage into young adulthood. By her own estimation, she was still very much the introverted woman, awkward and socially inept. She would occasionally date but was admittedly not boy crazy. She was not in any big rush to get married. She tended to stay within a small circle of like-minded friends, usually centered around the drama department, and just wait for the next big thing in her life to present itself.

It was also during her freshman year at Catholic University that Susan Sarandon, who by that time was jokingly referring to herself as "the oldest virgin," fell in love.

The meeting of Susan Tomalin and Chris Sarandon is shrouded in mystery. In the classic Hepburn sense, both have remained vague or downright evasive when it comes to particulars although Sarandon once admitted to *Rolling Stone* that he saw her perform in a freshman play.

Chris Sarandon was an attractive man with dark, brooding looks and classically chiseled features. He was an actor, serving out his grad-student duties, and three years Susan's senior. The buzz among the female students was that he was not seeing anyone and was thus eligible. The attraction between the two was immediate.

It was only a short leap from dating to becoming lovers. By the end of her freshman year, the couple were living together. And, as Sarandon is fond of saying, Chris Sarandon taught her everything there was to know. His enthusiasm for acting was contagious and Susan soon began to reexamine her attitude toward it and her talents. Where there was once indecisiveness, there was now a tentative but growing sense of enthusiasm and confidence.

SUSAN SARANDON

"When you're that age and you run into a grad student and he's showing you black and white movies and talking about art and poetry, it's really major," she said of her attraction to Sarandon in *Mirabella* magazine. "I was lucky to find Chris. He educated me and allowed me to make my own mistakes."

It was during this period that Sarandon also began to come to terms with her growing political and social activism.

Prior to college, her attitude, much in keeping with that of her parents, was knee-jerk conservative and centered around outdated notions of having to keep the Communists from our shores. But a lot had changed in the next few years.

Robert F. Kennedy and Martin Luther King Jr. had been assassinated during the time Sarandon was in college. The first reports indicating that Vietnam might not be the good fight were appearing in the earliest underground newspapers and on the op-ed pages of the braver mainstream press. For Sarandon, her political awakening coincided with a coming of age of the nation when issues were suddenly very clear.

Sarandon's growing sense of right and wrong and tradition be damned had found a conduit in the rising tide of liberal causes. Sarandon saw the times as her own personal rite of passage in which having an opinion was now considered, no matter how far out, a right rather than a privilege.

Sarandon took sides in 1964 when she began to participate in civil rights marches and anti–Vietnam War

44

demonstrations in and around the Washington, D.C., area and recalled in *Playboy* "being arrested a couple of times." Her philosophy at the time was pretty basic. Denying anyone their basic rights was wrong. Sarandon's feeling regarding the Vietnam War was that those who went to fight in Vietnam did not understand the reality of the situation because they were being given misinformation.

Cut and dried, perhaps a bit naive. But Sarandon was finding the idea of exercising her freedom of speech in a public arena an exhilarating experience.

"The point of being twenty was that you asked questions and you were irate and you wanted to change things and you believed you could. When I was twenty I was very mystical and spiritual. Back then I could really explore abstract questions and intuitive issues and go to the brink."

But, by her own admission, Susan's activist participation was regulated to the background. She was far from a firebrand and, in the most positive way, tended to be a follower rather than the outspoken critic she would become in later years.

Sarandon's relationship with Chris Sarandon was not considered out of the ordinary in 1967. The revolution of the sixties had paved the way for all kinds of social and sexual experimentation, and so, with the exception of the constant battles with her parents because of her "lack of morality" and the fact that Catholic University obviously frowned on the practice, Sarandon felt pretty comfortable in her living situation—which made it all the more surprising the day Chris and she decided to get married.

Neither one of them felt him- or herself to be the marrying kind and that marriage in general was on its way out. But, in a naive way, based more on their mutual friendship as much as their love, they decided to take the plunge.

"We decided it would make things easier for everybody if we got married," she told *Rolling Stone*. "I didn't think that much about it. The way I saw it, we would just renew every year. It was just one of those things you did for other people to make them comfortable. To my way of thinking, sex and love just went together."

In what many would consider a backhanded slap at convention, the couple were married on September 16, 1967, by the priest who headed the school's drama department. But rather than cementing her shaky relationship with her parents, the twenty-year-old Sarandon's marriage only made things worse.

"My marriage got me kicked out of the family," she recalled in *Mirabella* magazine.

Why remains a mystery with many theories but no solid answers. There had always been the tension surrounding the live-in relationship with Sarandon that even their finally getting married could not change. There was the notion, largely on her mother's part, that Susan had no ambition and, consequently, not much of a future. And finally, despite and perhaps because of her father's singing background, Susan's parents did not think highly of their eldest daughter marrying into the insecure lifestyle of an actor.

Sarandon graduated from Catholic University in 1968. Although she had a degree in drama, her interest in acting had not flowered into full-blown ambition. She would, in later years, proclaim that her years at Catholic University were more of a liberal arts jaunt (her theater arts classes were, in fact, more theory and literary) than anything else and that she had never really had what most would consider a formal acting lesson.

She readily admitted that she had gone at acting from a dilettante point of view and did not, in her wildest imagination, feel that any innate skills she might have developed along the way would result in any kind of career. Much like just about every other element of her life, Sarandon was not taking acting too seriously and basically looked upon the process and the pomp connected to acting as one big joke.

But that did not stop her from tagging along with her husband for a season at the Long Wharf Theater in Connecticut. For Sarandon, this accelerated course in production, in which new plays were turned out almost weekly, was her first true glimpse of the acting life (although she never had the occasion to act in a play opposite Chris Sarandon during this period).

While their time at the Long Wharf was an enlightening and creative period for the young couple, there was not much money coming out of the experience and so the Sarandons had to get about the business of earning a living. Susan's modeling credits in college eventually led to a contract with the famed Ford Modeling Agency. The Sarandons in Connecticut were living an idyllic quasi-bohemian existence.

Sarandon slid in and out of a domestic identity, puttering around in their small garden and baking bread. She could often be found sunning herself on a nearby beach. Chris Sarandon was finding regular work on Broadway and in regional theater in an informal circuit that took in Washington, D.C., Virginia, and Connecticut while Susan's expressive eyes and tight body were resulting in regular midlevel magazine and catalog work. There was no talk of children. The Sarandons were too caught up in their own worlds and their freedom to consider adding a child to the equation.

Chris's acting career was progressing at a steady pace and at one point he was asked to read for prominent New York agent Jane Oliver. Sarandon tagged along with her husband so "he would have a warm body to play against." The couple read for the agent from a selection of the play *The Hostage*. Oliver was suitably impressed with the audition and, in particular, Susan's unbridled passion. She strongly suggested that both of them come back and see her in the fall.

Chris and Susan did not need any more encouragement than that to move to the city. The couple were only in New York for five days when the agent called Chris with an audition for a small role in an equally small film called *Joe*.

Joe, starring Peter Boyle as a frustrated blue-collar worker whose response to a changing world is violence, was one of the first and most effective examinations of the ramifications of sixties counterculture, unlike the bloated bigger-budget studio efforts like *Getting Straight* and *The Strawberry Statement*.

Susan had no intention of auditioning but the casting director sized her up as a possible for the role of the central character's teenage daughter. Chris was surprised, and happily so, that his wife had landed a part. More highly evolved than most actors, he had no jealousy or ego problems. Which was why Sarandon, a still very young-looking twenty-one-year-old at the time, reluctantly agreed. But this would not be the typical audition.

"They asked me to do an improvisation," she recalled in an *American Film* interview. "I asked them what that was. They told me, I did it, and they gave me the job on the spot. I thought 'Gee, this seems easy; maybe I'll try acting for a while. Because, for me, it just seemed like anyone could be an actor."

But her elation was immediately followed by panic. "I remember calling my agent and telling her that I had been asked to play this part. And then I said, 'Now what do I do?' "

chapter three

"I DON'T KNOW IF PEOPLE CONSIDER ME A PAIN IN THE ASS"

Sarandon's often hectic days at the Long Wharf had not prepared her for the reality of low-budget filmmaking.

Joe was not a major studio production—and it showed. The hours were often predictably long. The work was often repetitive to the point of boredom as a surprising amount of detail and takes was being given priority over the actors' comfort. While the script had shown a primitive wit and intelligence, the intent, as those privy to dailies (the raw, unedited film footage) would attest, was that *Joe* was morphing into something quite powerful and unblinking in its look at the consequence of anger and unbridled freedom at the close of the sixties.

Sarandon was not looking at *Joe* as being great art or even the relatively important message picture it would turn out to be. To Sarandon, who was not easily impressed, it was a job, some money, some kicks, and a chance to hang out.

But Sarandon would end up learning a lot on the set of *Joe*. She learned that Peter Boyle, just beginning to make

51

his own breakthrough after a highly successful run in the improvisational group Second City, was a brilliant actor. She learned that she had natural instincts when it came to portraying a doped-out hippie chick, a depiction that was of Sarandon's own creation when director John Avildsen did not express the requisite knowledge of how a doped-out hippie chick would act. She was able to overcome her rigid Catholic upbringing in order to do her first nude scene, a relatively chaste bubble bath sequence.

And finally, Sarandon learned that Avildsen did not suffer actors lightly.

"I remember asking him a question," said Sarandon in *After Dark*. "He said, 'Susan, if I thought I would have to talk to you, I wouldn't have hired you.' "

But the wide-open guerrilla filmmaking process employed on the set of *Joe* allowed the young actress some elements of participation. Because of a lack of crew members, Sarandon did her own makeup and hair. And when a scene in which she was supposed to cry lacked any motivation, Sarandon took it upon herself to write a line of dialogue that made it all make sense. "I never knew actresses were supposed to do that," she chuckled in a *Playboy* interview.

The first time Sarandon saw herself on the big screen was more of an adolescent kick than a cathartic moment. If she had felt anything other than amused, it would not have been Sarandon.

That *Joe* would ultimately go on to become a critical and box-office success set the tone for Susan's future choices. Whether by luck or design, most likely the latter,

Sarandon would develop a knack for getting in on the ground floor of something that, like *The Rocky Horror Picture Show* and *Thelma & Louise*, would ultimately achieve some kind of notoriety or be surrounded in controversy.

In the case of *Joe*, the opening of the film occasioned both. The film was denounced in many quarters for its anger and violence. But the more farsighted members of the critical community also saw it as a primitive masterpiece, casting a look at the potentially dark side of the new revolution.

Sarandon's criterion for the roles she took would become even more instinctive as her career progressed. She would explain in those early years that she would take parts because she thought they would be fun, she liked the people involved in the project, or there was something in the role that frightened her or allowed her to stretch as an actress.

Critically, Sarandon was quietly recognized by reviewers as somebody with raw potential. A *Los Angeles Herald Examiner* review offered that "Susan Sarandon has an identifiable screen presence that convinces that she would be capable of much more." Likewise, the *Los Angeles Times* exclaimed, "Susan Sarandon as the gaunt, sad daughter is first rate." Adding to those early accolades, *Variety* offered, "Susan Sarandon is physically and emotionally right as the young daughter."

Sarandon came out of her film debut none the worse for wear and, in fact, quietly confident in her ability to play the acting game. And make no mistake, at that point, acting was far from a life decision. "All I know was that, after *Joe*, I thought, 'This was a funny business.'"

SUSAN SARANDON

A funny business that seemed instantly attracted to Sarandon's ballsy, don't-give-a-shit attitude and her good looks accentuated by her big, expressive eyes and long ringlets of hair. That, as an actress, Sarandon was still at that raw and undisciplined stage did not seem to dissuade too many filmmakers. For the next ten years, Sarandon landed every part she went up for.

While the actress will often admit that *Joe* had been a fluke, it had been a pivotal one in Sarandon's life. For while she had played the college game and was then playing the bohemian game on a fairly believable level, the reality was that Sarandon, at that point, was far from being hungry, driven, or passionate when it came to acting or just about anything else for that matter.

"I didn't even consider myself an actor for like the first ten years. I don't think I would have stayed looking for it if it hadn't just found me in those first five days of coming to New York. If it hadn't happened, I wouldn't have hung in. It's just not my nature, the whole suffering artists bit."

The last part of her statement would have to be considered a bit of dramatic license. For while Chris and Susan were far from rich, by actors' standards they were fairly well off—enough so that their New York apartment was bedecked with works of expressionist art and bits and pieces of exotic, modern furniture. A good bottle of wine was never out of the question and they could afford to eat out occasionally at a finer restaurant. The reality was that, on a material level, the couple was content.

While she remained quite the independent woman,

Sarandon was more than willing to let Chris be the star of the family and would encourage and support him at every turn. She considered *Joe* luck and nothing more.

But in the aftermath of *Joe*, Sarandon would find regular work. Her first big break came in television where she spent one year (1970–71) as Patrice Kahlman, the girl that everything bad seemed to happen to on the soap opera *A World Apart*. She would play essentially the same kind of role in 1972 on the soap opera *Search for Tomorrow*.

The soaps would prove a valuable tool in Sarandon's growing acting style. You were not given a lot of time or takes on a soap and so Susan learned the importance of getting it right the first time. And there was the never-ending treadmill of learning pages of new lines on a daily basis. For Sarandon it was grunt work of the most valuable kind, but the money was good enough so that she could quit modeling.

But while she was grateful for the on-the-job education, Sarandon, three years into a reluctant acting career, had no designs on settling into it. One could sense that she had actually felt sorry for those soap opera actors who proudly wore the badge of having been on their shows for twenty years or more. Sarandon most assuredly would not be one of them.

There would follow, in fairly rapid succession, a slew of "B" TV movies that included *The Apprentice* (1971), *The Haunting of Rosalind* (1973), *The Satan Murders* (1974), and *F. Scott Fitzgerald and the Last of the Belles* (1974). Sandwiched in and around these trifles were such guest-starring oddities as *Sesame Street* (1969), *Owen Marshall: Counselor at Law* (1971), and *Calucci's Department* (1973).

For Sarandon, these were all essentially on-the-job training as she began to slowly cultivate her own style of acting amid the chaos of low-budget films and the grind of series television. In the television movies, she was playing largely at clichés, the damsel in distress and the love interest. But what these television movies lacked in endearing quality, they more than made up for in fairly steady employment and lots of exposure. Those early series guest shots were a blur.

Make no mistake, there were some high points in the actress's dues-paying period. She landed a small role in the 1971 film *Lady Liberty*, which gave her the opportunity to watch Sophia Loren work. And in 1972, Sarandon made her debut Broadway appearance, playing Tricia Nixon in famed writer Gore Vidal's *An Evening with Richard Nixon and . . .* , and other roles.

Sarandon liked the surreal nature of the theater and the fact that it was one shot every night in front of a live audience. She also became good friends with Vidal. And she was having an enjoyable time at the expense of a politician she did not particularly care for. Unfortunately so-so reviews sank the production after only sixteen shows.

The Sarandons' marriage, which in later years Susan would describe as "a friendship marriage," was going along smoothly. The inevitable jealousies inherent in a two-actor marriage, especially in this one where Sarandon was making more money and doing seemingly more high-profile film and television work than her husband, were not an issue, the reason being that Chris Sarandon, in fact, was doing the classier work of the couple. He was gathering rave notices for his theater work, in such Broadway productions as *The Rothschilds* and *Two Gentlemen of Verona* and was about to break into films in a big way in the Al Pacino movie *Dog Day Afternoon*. On the surface, the relationship between Chris and Susan was strong.

But when the couple relocated to Hollywood in 1975, word began to get out that they were, in fact, separated. The rumor would turn out to be true.

The speculation that Sarandon's career was taking off while Chris's was stalled had driven a wedge of professional jealousy between the couple. A far more plausible explanation was that the couple, who admittedly had married quite young, had simply grown apart and fallen out of love. But since Chris and Susan were remaining mum on the topic, the first news that there had been a serious breech came when close friends discovered that Chris had moved out and gotten his own apartment.

Sarandon, who is fearless in discussing almost any subject, has never really opened up on the topic of her failed marriage.

"Our reasons for separating are our reasons and they are private," she once said. "I love Chris very much and we are still close friends. It was just time for me to grow."

Chris, in a 1976 *Elle* magazine interview, was even more succinct. "We are growing apart."

True to Sarandon's assertion, the separated couple

remained very good friends. During her downtime between work, Chris would regularly pick up Susan and
drive her to the unemployment office so she could get her
check. And neither felt a pressing need to divorce. Nor did
Susan feel it was necessary to give up the name of
Sarandon. And the reason was an enlightened sense of loy-
alty to what Chris had meant to her life.

"I thought he was responsible for my blossoming," she
candidly explained in *Mother Jones*. "I felt much more
attached to the person I became during my marriage than
to the person I'd been before. The name came from a dear
friend who happened to be my husband."

Chris also had no problem with Sarandon's decision,
acknowledging that his ex-wife had gained her reputation
with that name.

If Sarandon was truly sad at the end of her marriage, it
did not show. The actress in the early eighties had once
stated that she had increased the amount of work she was
doing so that it would get the same attention that her personal life was getting. One assumes that was her attitude a
decade earlier, because suddenly she was in demand and
she was saying yes to everything. Sarandon would be the
first to admit that at that point not a lot of thought went
into choosing those early roles.

Sarandon continued to find steady employment in
films that either came and went without much recognition
or were big-budget star-studded affairs that flopped or
underperformed.

In the former category was *Lovin' Molly*, in which she

had the opportunity to learn the ropes from veteran actors Anthony Perkins, Beau Bridges, and Blythe Danner. In the remake of *The Front Page* (1974) she played the fiancée of Jack Lemmon under the direction of famed filmmaker Billy Wilder, while in *The Great Waldo Pepper* (1975), a major disappointment starring Robert Redford, she played a small-town girl who falls under the spell of a barnstorming pilot and dies during a wing-walking stunt.

That none of these films was ultimately successful was of little concern to Sarandon. At that point, she was still looking upon acting as a game she was getting to play for pretty good money. She still saw her life and career as one big party and something she would never pursue at anything beyond a leisurely pace. But she was sensing that she would soon have to get serious about the profession that literally chose her.

Sarandon was in no hurry. She had spent a lot of time sliding easily through this early portion of her career on a wing and a prayer. To her way of thinking, there would, somehow, always be work. But there was a consistency in the work she was getting that was beginning to form an uncomfortable pattern.

She was playing fairly rote, untaxing clichés; the types of roles that were readily available to competent actors but that ultimately led to stereotyping and shortened careers. Sarandon finally saw her acting as a tool to take her to places and situations that were out of the norm and as an opportunity to be totally free. To accomplish those goals, she had to begin to take chances.

Sarandon has freely admitted that, during those early

years, Hollywood did not really know what to do with her. Although she could still believably play the young in-genue, there was much in the choices she was making that seemed to be leading her toward more character-oriented roles. But none of this concerned her. Sarandon was still at the stage where she was going with the flow. It was this attitude that led her to *The Rocky Horror Picture Show*.

The Rocky Horror Picture Show, a highly unorthodox send-up of horror films, rock music, and twisted sexuality, had been a sensation on the normally staid British stage and was, likewise, beginning to make inroads in America when a deal transferring the madness to film was inked. With its very British feel and its rock-and-roll attitude, *The Rocky Horror Picture Show* was considered a daring test of how much pop culture had impinged on society. But despite the enthusiasm, mainstream actors were shying away from the film project in droves, leaving the cast to such relative unknowns as Barry Bostwick and Meatloaf.

Sarandon was up for a part in what the industry con-sidered a prestige picture and was ready to go with that when she paid a visit to longtime friend and actor Tim Curry who had just signed on to play the transvestite mad scientist Dr. Frank 'n' Furter in the film after making the part his own in the U.S. theater run. Curry praised the script and eventually convinced Sarandon that it would be a lark to go in and audition for the role of wholesome Ohio bride Janet Weiss who is seduced by the evil Frank 'n' Furter and his demented minions and monsters.

Sarandon's agent and her closest confidants advised her

that *Rocky Horror* would not be a good career move. It was paying next to nothing and there was the real danger, whether the movie was successful or not, of her being typecast as a B movie bimbo. But Sarandon saw a lot of potential fun in the role and its requirement that she be able to sing, which would force her to stretch as an actress.

Sarandon, despite the fact that her father had sung professionally, had not been blessed with an even mediocre voice and had often been delicately advised by friends and associates that she could not carry a tune. The actress had taken it to heart and would often admit to breaking out in hives at the thought of even attempting to sing. When she got to the audition, the producers felt she had the right look and, for the moment, put aside the singing requirement and just asked Sarandon to read. In the various stage productions, Janet Weiss had been little more than a cardboard cut out and never what anyone would consider a funny character. But Sarandon's reading unexpectedly brought a dormant character, and a very funny one to boot, to life.

Sarandon's impression of the character Janet was a larger-than-life, *Saturday Night Live* version of every part she had played to that point. In her mind, Janet was a consummate bitch beneath the innocent image. She played the character that way during the audition and reduced the casting people to uncontrollable laughter.

Sarandon was asked to do some physical schtick and proved adept at the various walks, dance steps, and gyrations that would be required of Janet.

SUSAN SARANDON

"When the producers asked me to sing, I told them I didn't know how to," she explained in a *New York Times* interview. "I had never even hummed out loud. I was terrified. But I thought, 'You're really an idiot if you're afraid to sing.' Besides I thought that when the time came, they would give me the necessary drugs or liquor."

If she needed any further inducement, Sarandon liked the idea that she would be filming in London, her first opportunity to make a movie outside the United States. The actress was looking forward to making *The Rocky Horror Picture Show*. It would turn out, however, to be an experience not unlike her worst nightmare.

In recent years, Sarandon has hinted that the filming was marked by what she deemed "personal problems," although she has refused to go into specifics. There were the inevitable stories that Sarandon, with the exception of Curry, had immediately rubbed the largely British cast and crew the wrong way with her liberated attitude. What she would concede was that making the film was a constant physical and mental challenge.

It was December in London and Sarandon was running around half naked in a bra and half-slip and soaking wet. When she complained about the lack of heat on the soundstage, she was accused by the director of being self-indulgent. At one point during the filming, Sarandon came down with pneumonia. As filming wound down, the actress was in a constant state of exhaustion, marked by weight loss and constant colds and fever.

Not that the entire *Rocky Horror* experience was a

complete downer. Playing in this total fantasy environment was a constant challenge. The direction, despite the elaborate choreography, was fairly wide open and so Sarandon was, indeed, able to fine tune and manipulate her character as the production went along. She was the subject of a lot of good-natured ribbing when it came time for her to sing but, given the camp parameters of the film, Sarandon acquitted herself just fine. Sarandon found the cast highly supportive and tolerant of her mistakes.

The Rocky Horror Picture Show wrapped early in 1975. Susan Sarandon celebrated by having a nervous breakdown.

Sarandon's emotional disintegration manifested itself in a number of different ways. She lost her hearing, had memory lapses, and lost a lot of weight. She would have periods of extreme disorientation when she would look in a mirror and not know whom she was looking at. Sarandon began talking about herself in the third person.

The actress returned to the States and immediately checked herself into a hospital. But she did not like the way the hospital smelled and so she promptly checked herself out. But for the next nine months, Sarandon readily admits that she was in a desperate psychological state. She could not eat or sleep. She cried a lot.

At her lowest moments during what would be a nearly year-long period of depression, Sarandon felt that her world suddenly had no structure and that her lifelong notion of how her world worked was now being challenged. Rather than give in to the depression and roll into insanity with eyes wide open, the actress chose to meet her fears and to ride them and her depression to its inevitable conclusion. Sarandon, with the aid of a progressive doctor who did not believe in drugs or hospitalization, began to slowly climb out of her own personal hell.

Sarandon tended to dismiss those months as the result of an "identity crisis" brought about by a lifetime of trying to identify herself and her needs. But even in this tormented state of mind, a little voice inside Sarandon told her that this emotional collapse was all right for now but after a while it was going to become boring and so, through sheer strength of will, Sarandon pulled out of her depression and quite simply got on with her life.

Sarandon emerged from this dark period a somewhat changed woman. Although there was the need to work, the actress had decided that she would not be manipulated by the studio system and would do only the things that interested her. As if to make up for the years when she kept her true identity under wraps, Sarandon was now even more upfront and candid. In essence, the only thing her mental collapse had succeeded in killing was the very thing she wanted to get rid of—her insecurities. It was during this "coming out" that Sarandon once again took a look at the world around her and found a lot that she did not agree with and that scared her. Since her days protesting the war and marching for civil rights, Sarandon had been quick to state her opinion. But now she felt it was time to once again stand up and be counted. In the coming years, she would become a vocal supporter of nuclear disarmament, equal rights, and abortion rights. With her acting profile well below the radar, she would not have to contend with even the hint of celebrity baggage—which was fine with Sarandon.

Because, in her mind, acting and living had become two inseparable elements of her lifestyle. Through her emotional and professional trials, Sarandon had taken on a new level of strength, one that would allow her to do and feel things she had once thought she was incapable of doing and feeling.

At the height of this initial step toward activism Sarandon recalled stepping into the public eye for the first time. The occasion was a march in support of the Equal Rights Amendment that had culminated on the steps of the New York Public Library. Sarandon had gone in with the idea that she was there as a demonstrator and nothing more. But Bella Abzug and Marlo Thomas, the big celebrity names at the rally, recognized Sarandon's potential as a celebrity adjunct and, at one point, urged her to get up and speak. Sarandon was a reluctant public speaker but eventually got up and nervously spoke in front of the assembled television news crews. Sarandon would later recall in an interview with the *Progressive* that she learned a valuable activist lesson that day.

"The news reporters don't even tell what you've said half the time. All they do is show your picture for two seconds. It buys air time on television. That's why celebrities are present at rallies."

Sarandon's personal life also began to evolve. Although

still legally married to Chris Sarandon, Susan slowly began to get back into the dating world and, after a time, began a romantic relationship with writer-director John Leone. She remembered it as a "quick and uninhibited" relationship, not permanent but rather much in keeping with her philosophy of love and sex being interchangeable and not necessarily permanent.

Her relationship with Leone was far from the calm, reflective life she had had with Chris. Leone was a fiery, often volatile personality who would counter Sarandon's innate, nurturing nature with anger and negativity. She recalled that Leone put her through a lot of changes.

Sarandon acknowledges that, after a relatively calm relationship with Chris, dealing with the more volatile character of Leone was difficult. Her reaction to her lover's temperament was to withdraw. There would be long lapses of memory and bouts of disassociation.

For the first time, Sarandon did not have all the answers and so she went into therapy. And admittedly, the lessons she learned were hard ones. She learned that love does not automatically conquer all and that bad people and bad things can enter the life of good people. But she emerged from therapy a much tougher human being, one more capable of dealing with life.

Sarandon managed to turn this personal trial into a professional triumph. Leone had written and was set to direct a film called *The Great Smokey Roadblock* (aka *Elegant John and His Ladies*) and had managed to secure Henry Fonda for the lead. Sarandon landed a role as a good-hearted prostitute but, as time drew near for filming to begin, she also stepped into the breach as coproducer. "I just knew more about what was needed than most of the other people involved."

The filmmaking experience was the expected down-and-dirty B movie games. Lots of rolling trucks racing down country roads and cliché backwoods values combined to make this a fairly predictable outing. But Sarandon was attracted to the process and so the long hours and often less than ideal conditions were enjoyable with the extra added attraction of the actress getting to do a film with screen legend Fonda.

The Great Smokey Roadblock disappeared very quickly, as did Sarandon's relationship with Leone. Her career in a state of flux, and emotionally confused, Sarandon drifted into a number of forgettable or just plain bad films.

In Hollywood bad news travels fast. Sarandon's mental collapse had quickly become common knowledge and, in this, the first of what would be several long absences from her craft, she had slipped down a number of rungs on the ladder. Consequently, the pickings became slimmer.

In *Dragonfly* (1976), the potential of a young woman who becomes romantically involved with a man who has been recently released from a mental institution was scuttled by an ill-defined script and questionable costume and makeup choices. *Checkered Flag or Crash* (1976) was a mindless B action movie in which Sarandon and Larry Hagman took part in a thousand-mile road race through the jungle.

Admittedly these were not the best of times for

Sarandon. There was no high expectations for any of the work she was doing. She was occasionally battling bouts of loneliness. And finally, she was not finding a whole lot of glamour in what she was doing. But she was determined to move and the only direction she saw was up.

But the true test of Sarandon's mettle during that period was her participation in the film version of Sidney Sheldon's bloated potboiler, *The Other Side of Midnight*.

The actress sensed going in that the film treatment of the novel would never rise beyond the level of schlock and that it did have a definite aroma of bad movie surrounding it. But like every decision she made, Sarandon had a reason for jumping at *The Other Side of Midnight*, and that was she had to eat. In 1977 Sarandon was still another faceless element of the Hollywood acting hierarchy. She had proven herself reliable and quite an involving actress in the fluff she had appeared in but she was nowhere near bankable. And so if playing an alcoholic spurned wife of an air force pilot would put food on the table, so be it.

"It was never meant to be *Julia*," she laughingly explained to *Moviegoer*. "But when I read it, I thought, 'This is great; a woman gets to go from 17 to 35, from funny ingenue to alcoholic and wouldn't it be fun to tackle those changes.' There was something for me as an actress to hold onto there."

It was on the set of *The Other Side of Midnight* that Sarandon let her creative displeasure and frustration go for the first time. In a scene where she was about to experience her first sexual experience at the hands of actor John Beck, she complained long and loud about the incongruity of her standing almost completely naked while Beck advances on her in full military uniform. She complained to the director that logically Beck's character would at least be in a partial state of undress himself. Sarandon also complained that the scene was going to be shot completely in the dark, thus avoiding the reality of an uncomfortable first sexual experience. In both cases, Sarandon lost the war but succeeded in adding the latest chapter in her growing reputation as somebody who could be difficult.

"I don't know if people consider me a pain in the ass. I'm definitely not hard to work with unless I'm working with stupid people."

Sarandon's short fuse when it came to working with "stupid people" was on a par with her respect or lack of same when it came to confronting legends. Largely on the notoriety of *The Rocky Horror Picture Show*, Sarandon was invited on the *Tonight* show which, at the time, was hosted by television icon Johnny Carson, to help get the hype started on the still-filming *Other Side of Midnight*.

Also on the show that night was singer-activist Joan Baez. Sarandon found herself on common ground with Baez and, by association, found an easy target in the famously uptight Carson. Baez and Sarandon took turns needling the host and making fun of Carson who got so upset that he turned over the last half hour of the show to ragtime piano player Eubie Blake. Carson fumed behind his desk until the show's conclusion and then reportedly stormed off.

Sarandon recalled that Carson stormed off the moment the cameras went dark. *Tonight* show producer Freddy DeCordova came up to her and strongly suggested that it would be a good career move for Sarandon to make peace with Carson. Sarandon went to Carson's office and was told by his secretary that he was too busy to see her. Sarandon subsequently wrote Carson a note that was never acknowledged. But the actress recalled that it would be a long time before she would appear on the *Tonight* show again.

Midway through the filming of *The Other Side of Midnight*, Sarandon got wind of a much more offbeat project, *Pretty Baby*. This quiet, often disturbing tale centered around a photographer and an eleven-year-old prostitute in 1917 New Orleans had as its hook for Sarandon the admittedly secondary role of the girl's prostitute mother. Sarandon also liked the period nature of the film and the promised delicate handling of the more erotic moments.

There was also the film's pedigree to consider. This would be famed director Louis Malle's first American film after a distinguished career in Europe and his reputation as a powerful and insightful filmmaker intrigued the actress. Her costar in the film, Keith Carradine, had done some respectable work in *McCabe and Mrs. Miller* and the recently completed *Welcome to L.A.* There would be no small amount of controversy of the preteen Brooke Shields assaying a role that many would consider pornographic. Once again, Sarandon had been up for another role in a much safer film that, while offering her more money, would have continued to play her as the connect-the-dots ingenue.

She sensed the danger in *Pretty Baby*. The subject matter was explosive and Malle, despite a sterling reputation in Europe, was still a question mark to American audiences. But the risks and possibilities in the film excited her and so she willingly jumped into this chancy production.

"When I turned down a big movie to do *Pretty Baby*, my agents went crazy," she said in an *After Dark* interview. "They kept telling me how big this other movie was going to be. How did they know? So I just told them, 'Look, I did a big movie for you last year. So let me do this one now, okay?' "

Her agents gave in.

Sarandon arranged for a meeting with Louis Malle and was instantly drawn to the director as a highly creative and soulful personality. She came away from the interview in a positive frame of mind but, when she did not hear from Malle after a long time, she assumed she had not gotten the part and promptly forgot all about it.

"Suddenly I was asked to rush down to New Orleans. I was convinced that when I got off the plane, Louis would take one look at me and say, 'No, no . . . that's not the girl. I wanted Susan Blakley."

But Malle did indeed want Sarandon and as filming on *Pretty Baby* commenced, his gut reaction regarding the actress was confirmed. Malle would often be effusive in his praise for her "fresh, innocent, and flexible" approach to acting and the fact that Sarandon had "no system" when it came to practicing her craft. And by this time the report card on Sarandon was that, while she was still considered raw and slightly unorthodox in her acting approach, she could do a lot of the little things quite well. Which was exactly what Malle was looking for in the role of Hattie, somebody who could provide an emotional balance to the bizarre sense of reality he was trying to achieve with *Pretty Baby*.

By all accounts, *Pretty Baby* was not the easiest of shoots. There was the ongoing trauma of eleven-year-old Brooke Shields playing a child prostitute and having to do a nude scene. Shield's ever-present mother seemed, according to Sarandon, "not in good shape" emotionally. The primarily American crew had no idea who Malle was or how he worked, which led to a number of creative differences. There was also a lot of drinking on the set. Sarandon, for all her enthusiasm for the part, had some troubles early on in playing a prostitute.

But she eventually made the transition and remained a rock in her nuanced, multilayered portrayal of Hattie. In fact, Sarandon and costar Keith Carradine's work were the only things Malle could count on during the filming. In particular, he saw Sarandon as his professional and emotional anchor. Sarandon, likewise, looked upon her director as a man of quiet passion and integrity. Consequently it came as little surprise that Malle and Sarandon became lovers during the filming of *Pretty Baby*.

As was her trademark by this time, Sarandon would never speak at any length or in detail about her personal relationship with Malle, although it would later be discovered that Sarandon felt confident enough in the relationship with Malle to pencil in the name Lou to an equally temporary tattoo she put on her breast for a photo shoot. The director, in a 1978 *Cosmopolitan* interview, was only a bit more forthcoming.

"It is difficult for me to speak of Susan on a personal level," he said. "Because it makes everything I've said about her ability as an actress sound weird, as if my feeling for her colors my judgment. All I can say is that I love Susan very, very much and that I am happy that she is in my picture. Susan is my good luck."

But while mum on the subject of Malle, Sarandon's attachment was seemingly part and parcel of her growing personal and social philosophy about love and sex and a recurring defiance of her Catholic upbringing. Sarandon has often explained that her life "is ruled by Venus" and that there is an uninhibited streak in her love that is at once wild and passionate and yet monogamous on a very basic level. Hers has always been a bohemian way of performing in the arena of love and sex but in a manner that, at its core, is totally under control.

During the filming of *Pretty Baby*, Sarandon saw the completed *The Other Side of Midnight* for the first time. The actress's worst fears were confirmed. The movie was so unintentionally bad that she found herself laughing uncontrollably throughout the screening.

And she was not shy about telling the producers that when they asked her what she thought. She agreed to do some press for the film but would mention the movie only in passing and would spend her time talking about things she was interested in talking about. Surprisingly, this was okay with the studio. Susan's instincts about the film proved correct as it arrived in theaters to a critical drubbing and disastrous box office.

Pretty Baby was a whole other story. Sarandon was more than willing to meet the press on what she considered her breakout role. Critically and at the box office, the movie would turn out to be a moderate success. Malle was suddenly the new hot property in Hollywood, which assured Sarandon that their romance would not have to be carried out long distance.

That critics had continued to discover Sarandon's talents in the film was the proverbial icing on the cake. the *Los Angeles Times*, in a measured and somewhat cautious review, said, "Hers is much the best performance in the film." *After Dark* magazine chimed in with, "Susan Sarandon projects an appealing earthiness and careless full-blown beauty that is often breathtaking."

Sarandon was certain that her work in *Pretty Baby* would result in a rush of good scripts coming her way and that her days of questionable choices and erratic luck would be over. But when she read the script for *King of the Gypsies*, a family drama centered around a conflicted Gypsy and his family, based on the best-selling Peter Maas novel, Sarandon knew that she was about to roll the dice again. Although derived from superior source material, *King of the Gypsies* had the potential to be a large and unwieldy exercise. She saw few possibilities in the large ensemble cast for any one character to shine through.

In the character Rose, she immediately sensed she

would be wildly miscast: too small, too young, and too "white bread" for the part. But the risk involved in the part was also what attracted her. She knew she was either going to be very good in the film or really bad. To her way of thinking, there was no way she could play Rose halfway.

True to her prediction, *King of the Gypsies* was a struggle. She was hamstrung by a character who seemed duty bound to cliché and so it was a constant inner battle to bring even a shred of dimension to the character of Rose. She often felt that given the time and the freedom that there was a character worth finding and freshening up. But on the part of the filmmakers, there never seemed to be the inclination to try and draw something extra out of her.

King of the Gypsies turned out to be an entertaining and somewhat involving effort in which Sarandon received only mediocre notices. But, in hindsight, Sarandon would look back on the film and feel that this was the first time she was truly acting.

Sarandon was hopeful that her next choice, a relatively small film about love and romance called *Something Short of Paradise*, would put her back on track. But the film, which also starred David Steinberg, fell victim to less than fantastic direction and a ham-fisted script. *Something Short of Paradise* was quickly dismissed by critics as too talky and wildly pretentious.

The fate of *Something Short of Paradise* was a fitting climax to Susan Sarandon's first decade in front of the camera. With no particular career path in mind and nobody, at least on the surface, of any consequence in a management position to guide her, Sarandon was making scattershot choices, some of which would turn out, more through luck and the state of the cultural landscape, to have some lasting impact.

She was already hearing the buzz that, despite its failure upon release, *The Rocky Horror Picture Show* was unexpectedly proving wildly popular at scattered midnight screenings. *Pretty Baby* was also proving to be a well-remembered performance for Sarandon.

But to find some hint of potential greatness in these early choices would be quite a task because, with the possible exception of *Pretty Baby*, Sarandon was still learning the game of acting. And part of the reason was that she rarely had what would be considered a strong directing hand.

"I work best in a situation where I'm not in free fall," she explained in a *Washington Post* interview. "I like to know that somebody is giving me perimeters. I'm really freest when somebody's there, an adult telling me what they want me to say."

And so Sarandon ended the decade of the seventies pretty much where she started it: happy and secure in her personal life but struggling to break out professionally. But if she was concerned, Sarandon did not let on. She was convinced that things would happen in their own time.

While her professional life was on an upswing, her relationship with her parents continued to be strained. She would call and would occasionally go home for family gatherings. But what she would find was that she was basically dead to Phillip and Lenora. Her career never came up in conversations and any attempts she made to get them to open up about their feelings for the movies she had done were met with silence.

"My mother thinks I'm crazy and immoral," she sadly told *US*. "I cause them anger sometimes. But they know it's my life."

Susan Sarandon was about to turn thirty. She celebrated by quietly and amicably divorcing Chris Sarandon. Easily one of the friendliest Hollywood divorces on record, Chris and Susan would continue to remain good friends. Sarandon was now free to be with Malle without the figurative A for adultery pinned to her bosom. But what should have been a time for quiet celebration was also cause for reflection.

Sarandon's concept of divorce and officially ending a love relationship remained vague.

"He [Chris] was my first time out," she told *Playboy*. "Whatever changes we went through, we left behind our youth. In general, I don't see the end as the end."

But her attitude toward marriage was now set in stone.

"I no longer believe in marriage."

"SO I DECIDED TO LEARN ABOUT NICARAGUA"

On the surface, this seemed like quite the pronouncement about marriage.

Sarandon was far from mortally wounded by her first brushes with love and romance and, to the casual observer, her giving up on the institution so quickly seemed merely the extension of her dramatic nature and something that would turn around in time. After all, her life with Malle was good and she might easily want to make the relationship permanent at some point. But the actress remained insistent that she was serious and perhaps more than a little commitment phobic about avoiding the institution of marriage a second time.

But, she would often exclaim, a failed marriage did not put her off the idea of falling in love again and that a relationship or relationships would most certainly happen when the time and chemistry were right.

"I've pretty much accepted the fact that I feel alone much of the time and there's a big chance that I'll be alone. But I still think there's someone out there who shares my perspective and need for excellence and wants some kind of dignity."

Her "feeling alone" remarks were admittedly in line with her theatrical Garbo-like attitude. The fact of the matter was that she had gathered a rather large and informal group of friends that she would congregate with over dinner or at parties. And, although the reality of the business meant that she and Malle would often be apart, when they were together she found herself quite happy.

But truth be known, Susan did cherish her time alone with a book or with her thoughts. So while she was not in the frame of mind to fall in love, mentally and spiritually she was hardly alone during her postmarriage and first rough relationships period.

However, at the time there were more pressing issues for Sarandon than her love life. Her career had plateaued with the success of *Pretty Baby* and her growing cult following as a result of *The Rocky Horror Picture Show*. There had, of course, been those clinkers that came with paying dues and the subtle machinations of the film-making process. Along the way, Sarandon had grown into the idea of acting as a serious and, yes, honorable profession. She reasoned that she would have to be smarter and a bit choosier in the future—because that's what a serious actress was about.

Despite such pronouncements, however, Sarandon continued to rely more on her gut reaction rather than any notion of business acumen when it came to choosing her roles. Consequently she was constantly at odds with her often exasperated agents who would routinely watch as their client turned down higher-profile, safe main-stream projects in favor of riskier parts in questionable pictures. And then there were those times when Sarandon took their advice.

Sarandon had nothing more than a good feeling to go on about her next picture, *Loving Couples*. A comedic romp about disintegrating marriages and partner swap-ping that was much in the tradition of *Bob & Carol & Ted & Alice*, the script struck a nerve with the actress's growing sense of social and sexual awareness in her own life. It offered the opportunity to work with established actors Shirley MacLaine and James Coburn and a little known but reportedly workmanlike director in Jack Smight. This, she reasoned in line with her new career-oriented attitude, could get her out of the rut of what she felt was a number of solid performances in mediocre films.

Loving Couples was not to be.

The script that had enticed Sarandon in the first place was thrown out during the second day of rehearsals and the first writer dismissed. A quick rewrite transformed what had been a solid, four-person character study into a less substantial and in the end highly predictable tale of a woman juggling two men.

This was not the movie Sarandon had signed on for and, she reasoned, appearing in it under these circum-stances would only do her career more harm than good. For the first time in her relatively young career, Sarandon felt like she had no control. And so, against her agent's advice, she walked into the producers' offices and told them she was quitting the film. Sarandon was not ready for the producers' response.

In a not-too-veiled threat, Sarandon was informed that her professional life would become very difficult if she walked off the film at that point.

Her first brush with Hollywood hardball tactics was an eye-opening experience. She immediately thought of walking anyway and fighting the producers in court—and just as quickly realized that since she barely had the rent, how was she going to afford a lawyer? Sarandon had no idea what the producers could actually do to her but she sensed that it would be wise to back down, at least for the moment.

Adding insult to the not-too-implied threat was the fact that Sarandon did not even have a wardrobe for the picture. When she complained, the costume designer for Shirley MacLaine was brought to Sarandon who went into great detail about her character and the type of clothes she would wear. The designer went away and came back one day before filming began with a lot of clothes—none of which fit. Sarandon would later discover that they were MacLaine's leftovers.

Sarandon angrily turned to her agent for help in this rapidly disintegrating situation but was not satisfied with his not-too-subtle suggestion that she just close her mouth and do the film. She left the agent shortly after completing *Loving Couples* and went her own way.

Loving Couples had little success in its final, compromised form. Susan was not bothered too much by the mixed reviews of her performance, figuring a movie that relatively few people would see could hardly hurt her career.

Her frustration with *Loving Couples* and the sudden, inexplicable loss of confidence in her abilities as an actress caused Sarandon to back off and retrench. That she felt less of an actress was more the accumulation of mediocre and underperforming films in the wake of her supposed breakthrough in *Pretty Baby* than any true erosion of her talent. That she was feeling battle-fatigued and frustrated was an indisputable fact. The last thing she wanted at this point was to simply take another in what had become a largely unrewarding series of jobs just for the sake of working.

Sarandon's answer was to retreat from what she perceived as the patently false and hypocritical Hollywood scene and to go to New York where she attempted to reestablish her reputation in what she felt was the much purer environment of the theater. Not that the film offers had stopped coming in. Sarandon had hooked up with another agent and, in rapid succession, had turned down lucrative paydays in any number of pictures on the grounds that they would do nothing to enhance her reputation as an actress.

Instead, she chose to do an obscure off-Broadway play entitled *A Coupla White Chicks Sitting Around Talking*, a two-woman exercise in angst opposite veteran actress Eileen Brennan. Susan was drawn to the simplicity of the production, the opportunity to do something a bit edgy and out of character. The respect she had for her costar was a major inducement and, as an off-Broadway production, the wounds would not be too deep if she fell on her ass.

During rehearsals, Sarandon began to feel the excitement she had not really experienced since the early stages of her career. The promised chemistry between herself and Brennan was much in evidence. Sarandon was feeling challenged by the intensity of the words and the stark tension apparent in the simple story. She had always been told that there was a world of difference between theater and film, and she sensed that was what she was feeling.

From the opening night audiences were treated to Sarandon in a stark, raw performance that stripped away any hint of pretense and Hollywood gloss. To a large degree, *White Chicks* reflected a lot of the emotional baggage of the actress's real life. And in that sense, Sarandon had gotten quite good at playing herself.

The play was a critical success, with many reviewers noting that after what could only be described as an up-and-down film career, Sarandon had found her niche, both comic and serious, in the role of a stressed-out housewife.

Time applauded her performance by saying, "Sarandon arcs over and under her emotional crises like a dolphin." *Newsweek* was equally praiseworthy, "What makes it go is the delicious acting of Susan Sarandon. Her Maude moves from comic catatonia to equally comic hysteria."

Sarandon has looked back on *White Chicks* as both an ego boost and the reason she got into acting. "This is what I do, it pleases me and obviously I'm good."

Flushed with the success of a long run in *White Chicks*, Sarandon plunged headlong into the more artistic side of her craft; forming an improvisational acting workshop with Richard Dreyfuss, Carol Kane, Peter Boyle, Andre Gregory, and others where she found new strength in cutting-edge acting techniques and productions.

Sarandon's "New York period" had the potential to be both a career maker and a career changer. There was more than enough opportunities in the burgeoning early eighties theater to insure Sarandon an endless list of good roles in quality productions. Her film career was beginning to pale in her mind when stacked up against her newfound heaven on Broadway. One more solid role and Hollywood could have lost her forever. But Sarandon was smart enough to realize that film was ultimately where she would find mass acceptance and so, while leery of the process, she never considered giving up on Hollywood altogether.

During this period, Sarandon was once again coaxed back into films when her lover, Louis Malle, suggested that she play the part of a frustrated waitress and wanna-be croupier who falls in love with an aging Mafioso (Burt Lancaster) in *Atlantic City*. Sarandon was delighted with the unorthodox, out of kilter, and, yes, slightly older character as well as the opportunity to work with screen legend Lancaster. And it went without saying that anything Malle was involved in would be a creatively satisfying experience— but one that would be bittersweet.

For while Sarandon, under Malle's direction, was turning in a performance that would not only change Hollywood's perception of her but also garner her legitimacy with her first Oscar nomination, it was becoming clear to Sarandon that the romantic fires were beginning to cool. Again, there were many reasons for the end of the relationship.

The pair had spent a lot of time apart, a surefire relationship killer. There were also the expected rumors that Malle had used their time apart to begin seeing another woman. Whatever the reason, the extra tension between the two did nothing to diminish a landmark performance by Sarandon who was completely focused on getting this ultimately doomed personality down on film.

The scenes between Sarandon and Lancaster, quiet and yet containing a complex sense of longing, were the perfect complement to this quietly told tale. Both actors realized that they were in a rare environment in which dialogue and emotion were everything, and brought some exceptional moments to the table. The consensus among those on the set was that Sarandon, in particular, was turning in a performance comparable to and possibly better than her turn in *Pretty Baby*.

Shortly after the completion of *Atlantic City*, Sarandon and Malle parted. Sarandon felt that the time apart and, in particular, Malle's decision to edit *Atlantic City* in Europe while Sarandon stayed in New York to pursue theater work ultimately doomed their relationship. If Sarandon thought she was going to be able to go away and deal with the breakup in private, she was mistaken. Sarandon would become the subject of some tabloid-style gossip when, shortly after their breakup, Malle became involved with another actress, Candice Bergen, whom he would eventually marry in 1980. But Sarandon, while never divulging her personal feelings about the relationship and the breakup to any great degree, did diplomatically acknowledge that she would be forever grateful to Malle for helping her to feel more comfortable with herself as an actress.

However, Sarandon would, in the wake of their breakup, often get defensive at the speculation that her career might have gone smoother and she might have risen in the Hollywood ranks faster if the relationship with Malle had endured. She would acknowledge the fact that his career might well have benefited from his working with her but would eventually concede that her time with Malle was well spent and an education.

There would be indications in later years that the break with Malle was a lot rougher than she had initially let on. She hinted in a *Playboy* interview that the breakup was Malle's doing and not hers. She also indicated years after the split that they had not spoken and that she did not think of Malle and her as friends. But she also indicated that she held no grudges and that she valued their time together, no matter how frustrating and intense it would often get, and that she had learned much about herself during her time with the director.

"I deal with reality, the feelings I have at the moment," she once explained in *Cosmopolitan*. "And then I go on from there."

Sarandon's words were further evidence of a growing personal philosophy in which love and sex translated into just another life experience to be savored for whatever length of time, and then to move onto the next. Her words, to the casual observer, might have seemed cynical and bitter but to those who knew Sarandon, they were actually the latest chapter of an ongoing philosophical manifesto that the actress was learning to live by.

Sarandon's breakup with Malle was personal. But it did not stop the actress from doing her professional duty on behalf of *Atlantic City*. With Malle back in Paris and Lancaster reluctant to do press, it fell to Sarandon to plug the film to the media. It was the first time Sarandon had been left to carry the press duties alone and, as she wandered in and out of television studios and dealt with a seemingly endless and often faceless series of talk-show hosts, she had to laugh at the process and her part in it.

"You try to talk about things you really care about," she told *Rolling Stone*, "not just bullshit and, by the time you've said everything you care about thirty-five times, it sounds like bullshit."

Reviewers, despite the stature of a first-rate performance by Lancaster and Malle's delicate turn as director, continued to take notice of Sarandon's acting skills in *Atlantic City*. The *Village Voice*, in a rave notice, highlighted the actress by saying, "The creative mixture of shrewdness, vulnerability, and sensuality that went into Sarandon's performance came as a breath of fresh air." *Newsweek* said, "Sarandon is touching and funny, a truly fresh performance." *Time* allowed as, "There is a core of strength in her. She evokes sympathy without asking for pity."

While none of this was a startling revelation, the good notices, coupled with her recent triumph in *White Chicks*, went a long way toward restoring her confidence in herself as an actress. With her personal life on the rocks, Sarandon felt she needed something positive to hold onto. She was now, pure and simple, focused in her acting life.

At this juncture, Sarandon had already decided to make New York her home. Her reasoning was simple. New York, in its people, energy, and all its manifestations, was a real, life-enriching environment.

Sarandon continued to devote time to her acting workshop throughout 1981 and into 1982. Some scripts were offered but were of little interest. One offer she laughingly dismissed was the opportunity to reprise her *Rocky Horror Picture Show* role of Janet Weiss in the much-hyped but finally just plain bad (as opposed to camp) sequel, *Shock Treatment*.

Her one screen role during this period was in a small, well-received movie for television entitled *Who Am I This Time?* The film, in which two shy people can express their love for each other only through their roles in a theater production, costarred Christopher Walken. Sarandon and Walken were very much into the method acting of this role and continued to date for a time after the completion of the film. Sarandon, who at this point was not looking for a committed relationship, also dated actors Tom Noonan and Kevin Kline during this period.

That she would date almost exclusively actors was predictable. This was her world and actors were seemingly the only eligible men around. That dating an actor usually resulted in ego, volatility, and time apart that would ultimately doom the relationship did not concern Sarandon. While never what anyone would consider a party girl, Sarandon was, at that point, just looking for a good time more than a lasting relationship.

Dating in general was turning into a tricky proposition for Sarandon. She was at a point in her life when she was more interested in having friends than lovers. Unfortunately the men she invariably came in contact with tended to reject her as a friend and were only interested in her sexually. She was frustrated as she explained to *Playboy* how a man was pursuing her sexually and refusing her offer of friendship. Finally, to test his intent, she agreed to sleep with him once but then would never see him again. The man readily agreed to the sex. Sarandon was angry and yes, for the record, did not have sex with this man.

"I thought, 'What a jerk! You're not smart enough to see that you're throwing away an incredible resource in exchange for one night.' "

Toward the end of 1982, Sarandon once again took to the stage in the physically and emotionally demanding play *Extremities*, in which her character turns the tables on a rapist. She would admit that only a crazy person would spend her time and ultimately risk her reputation on an off-Broadway play that was not only obscure but extremely unpleasant.

Initially Sarandon had some problems with *Extremities*'s extreme level of violence and the fact that she would appear in her underwear throughout most of the play. But Sarandon ultimately put aside those concerns and, reasoning that the subject matter was important and that it was the rare production that offered anything meaningful, took the leap.

During her run with the play, Sarandon overcame a nightly battering that resulted in a black eye, bloody noses, and all manner of bumps and bruises to turn in a raw, primitive performance that had critics handing out the kind of raves that easily rivaled her reception in *White Chicks*.

A *New York Times* reviewer, attesting to her power on stage, said, "The director directs all the scenes like hand grenades and, in particular, Susan Sarandon lobs them with precision."

The inherent controversy of *Extremities* fanned the flames of rape awareness in the city. So many questions were being asked that, at the suggestion of a local rape counseling group, the producer of the play arranged to have discussion sessions after selected performances of the play in which audience members were joined by the actors and rape crisis counselors. In all, a dozen such meetings were held. Sarandon attended and spoke at every one.

And it was during these meetings that Sarandon admitted that she had once been raped by someone she had known.

"I didn't know it was rape at the time," she said in a candid 1984 *Cosmopolitan* interview. "But I know it now. A lot of rapes happen that way, you're pressured into it by someone and you're too young and dumb to know that the man was the one who did something brutal and wrong."

Sarandon would rarely bring up the incident in later years and then couched the incident in vague terms other than rape. But the incident obviously has continued to resonate with the actress and, most likely, was a driving force in her becoming involved in women's rights issues.

Sarandon's reputation as a wild, free spirit made her love life or alleged love life a favorite topic among gossip columnists. During the early eighties, Sarandon fueled the speculation by readily admitting that there was a man in her life but refused to name him. Among the prime suspects regularly trotted out in the newspapers were Art Garfunkel, Richard Gere, and *Extremities* producer Chris Gero. Playfully, Sarandon would only offer that her mystery beau was a good cook, had a good sense of humor, and he respected her need to sometimes be alone. What is known is that the relationship, like others, ran its course and Sarandon was once again alone.

It was during this period that Susan Sarandon discovered AIDS. Not that she was totally ignorant of the disease. She could not be around actors, many of whom were openly gay, and not have heard of what was then being called "the gay cancer." But in the early eighties, AIDS was a disease that had not yet become a high-profile, cause célèbre and so if it was discussed at all, it was in whispers and in the shadows. In 1982, AIDS struck close to home for Sarandon.

Bobby Christian and Sarandon had become close friends years earlier when both had worked together in the play *An Evening with Richard Nixon and* . . . . When Christian contracted AIDS, Sarandon saw firsthand the suffering and the ignorance surrounding the disease. She painfully recalled that Christian died alone and in isolation because he did not want even his closest friends and family to know he had AIDS. Watching her friend dying galvanized Sarandon into action.

"After he died, I went to one of the very first anti-AIDS marches from Sheridan Square to New York's City Hall," she remembered in an interview with the *Progressive*. "I was the only woman there and everyone was quite shocked to see me. To me it seemed like a normal thing. I didn't question it for a second. I was just going to walk in memory of my friend."

The rally ended up at city hall and Sarandon was asked to speak. It was at that moment that the actress realized, despite watching her close friend die from AIDS, that she really knew nothing about the disease. Sarandon vaguely remembered her speech that day being more emotional than fact-based. But she vowed that from that day forward, she would not get involved in any cause that she did not first know inside and out.

Professionally, Sarandon continued to struggle. Her growing reputation as being difficult and outspoken notwithstanding, Sarandon was considered a topflight actress who was most certainly only one major role away from stardom. And because of that she would regularly be courted by big-name agents who were convinced they could help the actress turn the corner—if only she would play by their rules. Sarandon recalled a couple of those situations in *Rolling Stone* in 1981.

SUSAN SARANDON

Superagent Jay Bernstein, who had guided Farrah Faw-cett to small-screen stardom in *Charlie's Angels*, felt Sarandon had all the makings of the next Jane Fonda. But he warned her upfront that their relationship would be rocky if she was going to continue to be politically out-spoken and that championing causes like AIDS would hurt her in the eyes of conservative Hollywood. Sarandon appreciated his candor and went elsewhere.

For a short period of time, she was a client of agent-producer Aaron Russo. But his philosophy of putting her in a commercial film, no matter what the quality, ran afoul of Sarandon's artistic attitudes and so they quickly parted company.

Sarandon was shell-shocked and cynical at the suddenly dwindling possibilities in her professional life. While she was willing to shoulder some of the blame, she was not going to let Hollywood off so easily. She felt that the highly irrational nature of the business had conspired to prevent her from building a consistent body of good work and, at her most cynical, she was feeling that there was no justice to it.

But Sarandon had come too far to just pack it in and so, confident that things could only get better, she pushed on.

The actress returned to the big screen in 1981 with quirky director Paul Mazursky's modern retelling of Shakespeare's last play *Tempest*. From its inception, the director felt that Sarandon would be perfect in the role of Aretha, the modern-day equivalent of Ariel, the mistress to John Cassavetes's transplanted New Yorker figure of Prospero. "I didn't know her that well," remembered

Mazursky. "But I believed Susan was mature enough to meet someone and get involved with him very quickly. I knew she would not be afraid."

That the role of Aretha seemed to mirror Sarandon's own philosophy about sex and love made the part all the more attractive to the actress. She was also quite flattered that Mazursky had pursued her for nearly a year before she agreed to do the film. And she could not pass on the opportunity to act opposite John Cassavetes, an actor she greatly admired.

Unfortunately, Sarandon made the mistake of not reading the script too closely before reporting to the set for the beginning of filming. When she did, she discovered that the role was nothing more than a sexual cipher whose promiscuous nature ran contrary to Sarandon's notion of a liberated woman whose entire life was not designed around men.

And by association she also discovered that her perspective on the film and Mazursky's were definitely very different. In hindsight, she would later recall that she felt that the director was very limited by his own experience in how he saw women and, consequently, would force her to play directly opposite what she considered the logical emotions of the character. Sarandon would later acknowledge that she felt "very inhibited by the perimeters within which I had to function."

"I just got sick," she remembered. "This woman was so uninteresting. All she wanted to do was get laid."

Sarandon decided that she had to get out of this film,

no matter the cost to her already tarnished reputation. She took the drastic step of cutting off all her hair, figuring that Mazursky would fire her on the spot. But the director stood fast in his decision to not let her out of her contract, insisting she was the only one who could play the part.

Frantic, Sarandon went to costar John Cassavetes's room where she repeated her unhappiness with the script. Cassavetes jokingly said that he would break her legs if she tried to leave. He also assured her that they should not be worried about the script and that they should just have fun.

And once filming commenced, Sarandon did, indeed, find a lot to keep her interested. The chemistry was good between her and Cassavetes and there turned out to be a strangely subtle improvisational quality to Mazursky's direction that allowed her to indeed give her character the twists she felt it needed to be a more substantial role. But *Tempest* was not a perfect fit.

Sarandon remembered in a 1982 *Moviegoer* interview that she and Mazursky "fought" constantly and that in the end "I wound up playing it his way." But her respect for his vision and the ability to get that vision to the screen overcame any negative feelings about the character she was playing, especially when her persistent arguing with Mazursky did result in his adding some elements to the Aretha character that ultimately did give her more substance.

For all her trepidation, Sarandon's work in *Tempest* stands out in a solid second tier of performances following *Pretty Baby* and *Atlantic City*. *Tempest* received mixed reviews upon its release but most were typical of the sentiment of *Entertainment Today*, which said, "Susan Sarandon is always earthy and erotic."

Sarandon's personal life was dealt a telling blow in 1983 when she discovered that she had endometriosis, a disorder that affects fertility. Sarandon was told that she would not be able to bear children unless she underwent a series of operations. Sarandon gave it much thought before deciding against the procedures. "I had so many nieces and nephews at that point, I thought, I'll just be Auntie Mame."

But while she put up a confident front, there were many in her inner circle who were convinced that Sarandon was taking the news a lot harder than she was letting on. Sarandon had never been big on things being final. That fate had arbitrarily slammed the door shut on her ever having children alternately angered, frustrated, and saddened her.

Professionally, despite a growing résumé of quirky and often compelling work, Sarandon continued to struggle. She was in a cycle of bad or questionable offers that her pride would not let her accept. There was also frustration at invariably not getting a shot at the good parts she knew were available but not for her. She was always broke and always looking for work. But even at her most dire moments, she was instinctively ready to put her views ahead of her career.

A prime example came in 1983 when she was put up for a role in the latest Clint Eastwood vehicle, *Tightrope*. Sarandon was troubled by this detective thriller's correlation between sex and violence and had never really been a fan of testosterone-driven action films that always painted the women as love interests or victims.

"But I was completely broke and I was desperate to work and so I met with him (Eastwood)," she recalled in the *Los Angeles Times*. "I said, 'Aren't you worried when your character starts to do some of this stuff, that it's going to have a link between sex and violence and treating women badly?' He said, 'I don't think it's my job to worry about that. I'm an actor.' "

Sarandon turned down the role. Her integrity was intact but her bank account was empty.

The actress continued to go with her instincts when it came to film roles and continued to suffer erratic results. She jumped into *The Hunger*, a bisexual vampire tale directed by Tony Scott and costarring Catherine Deneuve and rock-star-turned-actor David Bowie.

Making this movie was like returning to the world of *Rocky Horror* for the actress. There was a very gothic-hip quality to the film that Sarandon found amusing. Much of what went on in the film required her to play it straight in an over-the-top, often surreal situation which Sarandon found a quirky challenge. Plus she would be working with some cool people and, in the case of Deneuve, someone she greatly admired.

The highlights for Sarandon were a soft-focus lesbian love scene (her first) with Deneuve and a short real-life romance with Bowie after the completion of the film. *The Hunger* received so-so reviews but, owing to a studio shakeup, was barely seen. *The Hunger*, much like *The Rocky Horror Picture Show*, would go on to become a cult item due, in large part, to Sarandon's love scene.

But it would be a film in which Sarandon grew as a person and a performer who would not back down in the face of perceived stupidity or ignorance. This was Sarandon's first sex scene as well as her first lesbian sex scene. The actress had no problem with it and felt comfortable with Deneuve whom she was finding a joy to work with. But what she was not comfortable with was the way the now-infamous scene had been written.

In the original draft of the script, Sarandon's character was drunk and than taken by Deneuve. Sarandon objected vehemently to the element of victimization in the scene. Director Scott was amenable to some change and so that scene was dutifully rewritten—but into an equally repulsive sequence in which the pair are simply talking and the next thing you see is the couple in bed actively engaged in sex. The reworking did not ring true to her either. Sarandon finally took the bull by the horns and made up her own scene in which she spills something on her blouse, hands the blouse to Deneuve who hands her something else to wear, and, in the process of that exchange, they touch for the first time. She would remember that the actual scenes in bed with Deneuve were fairly easy to do and that her initial bout of nerves had evaporated the moment the pair got into bed.

"I've always had my mouth open," Sarandon told *Playboy* regarding her propensity for making suggestions.

"Whether people listen to me or not, I don't know. But I've always made suggestions."

Sarandon would end up making a few converts among reviewers even with this questionable choice. *Los Angeles Magazine* gave a spirited, occasionally tongue-in-cheek account of the film and said of Sarandon, "Sarandon possesses an ethereal beauty that attacks an area somewhere deep within the brain stem, a beauty that goes straight into the subconscious."

The film did offer Sarandon the opportunity to address her own liberal attitude toward sexuality in the love scene with Deneuve. She recalled the experience in a 1999 issue of the *Lesbian News*.

"I definitely was the one who said, you know, I shouldn't be drunk. What's the point? I mean if you're gonna choose to go to bed with a woman and its Catherine Deneuve, you shouldn't be drunk. When you're doing a scene that's sexual, what's interesting is what leads up to it and what happens afterward. Everybody knows what happens in between."

Sarandon next teamed with old friend Richard Dreyfuss in *The Buddy System* as two friends who are maneuvered into a love relationship but who then decide they were better friends than lovers. Sarandon liked the approach *The Buddy System* took in presenting love and romance in comedic terms and she had a ball working with Dreyfuss. But unfortunately, this film also received a marginal release due to studio executive changes, so it quickly disappeared.

"So I Decided to Learn About Nicaragua"

After the less than stellar results of *The Hunger* and *The Buddy System*, Sarandon began to take stock of herself as an actress in the Hollywood pecking order and she came to a harsh truth: She was, despite stellar work in *Pretty Baby*, *Atlantic City*, and, to a lesser degree, *Tempest*, considered Hollywood's equivalent of a pinch hitter. She felt she was in a period in her career where she was being cast in films where either the part was not very good, the original choice for the part had dropped out, or they simply could not find anybody else to cast.

Despite having a career that, to that point, was consistent only by its inconsistency, Sarandon, now in her mid-thirties, was now beginning to think of herself as more of a leading lady. But she maintained that it was the challenge of the role that was her ongoing concern. In the overall scheme of things, Sarandon much preferred having four dynamic scenes that affect the action to just holding the arm of the leading man while he tries to figure out what his problem is.

And, in looking back on her early body of work, she readily admitted that fear had guided her most daring and ultimately most successful choices. "Every traumatic thing I've ever been through, personal, professional, whatever, has always, down the line, paid off somehow. I consider myself lucky."

But rather than dismissing it all as dumb luck, Sarandon could only look at her career at this point as "strange." And, as she would readily admit, a lot of it was of her own doing. For every questionable role she would accept,

Sarandon would inexplicably find a reason to turn down a seemingly worthy project. One of her most infamous rejections during this period was what would ultimately become the box-office smash *Romancing the Stone*.

Sarandon did not believe that she was, subconsciously, trying to sabotage her career. She was just trying to figure out what kind of career she should have. The quirky parts would keep her working but, most likely, would keep her mired in underappreciated obscurity. To attempt to become a legitimate leading lady would lead to necessary compromises which Sarandon did not believe she was ready to do.

With the quality of film roles declining, Sarandon turned introspective. Her political and social ideals became more important.

Sarandon began to network with ordinary people rather than celebrities and learned about the rest of her world. And what she found was not often pleasant. Sarandon was particularly struck by the reports of war and atrocities being carried out in Central America and, in particular, America's involvement in the ongoing strife in Nicaragua between the Contras and the Sandinistas. In Nicaragua, Sarandon saw a chance to help, and a cause that, in its own way, hit close to home.

"I have two brothers of draft age and I spend lots of money on taxes and I think that our policies of intervention lead to big wars. So I decided to learn about Nicaragua."

She became an avid reader of sections of the *New York Times* that she used to give only a cursory look. She paid close attention to CNN and its extensive coverage of Central American matters. Sarandon began to attend rallies, primarily as an observer, to find out exactly who was out there and what they were talking about.

Her celebrity helped her get into the enclave of many left-wing groups. And once they saw that Sarandon was serious about learning and not just another actor researching a role, she was welcome. Slowly the political landscape as it pertained to Nicaragua and U.S. involvement began to crystallize for the actress. She instinctively knew which side she was on.

Also in 1983, Sarandon narrated a PBS documentary about the history of American involvement in Nicaragua entitled *Talking Nicaragua*, which further raised her curiosity about what was really going on in this country that was rarely talked about by the media. Although an obvious liberal, Sarandon found herself, during the making of *Talking Nicaragua*, taking great pains to find out both sides of the story. She was particularly interested in the facts that supported or disproved the obvious arguments on both sides. Sarandon continued to dig deep into the history of the country and the ongoing war that, in most parts of the world, would not rate more than a few paragraphs on the back page of a newspaper.

Through her involvement in *Talking Nicaragua* Sarandon made the acquaintance of Dr. Myrna Cunningham. Cunningham was a Nicaraguan activist who had suffered the real horrors of war when she had been kidnapped and raped by the Contras. She held Sarandon spellbound with her tales of families being torn apart by the conflicts in the

Central American country. At the end of their talks, Cunningham would inevitably make the offer to Sarandon to come to Nicaragua and see for herself. Sarandon was tempted but not yet ready.

Adding to her political education, Sarandon became aware of an organization of Nicaraguan women called the Committee of Mothers of Heroes and Martyrs. The group, whose members had all lost a child or loved one in the Nicaraguan conflict, was attempting to get information to the U.S. government about the real horrors of the conflict by contacting politically and socially minded women in the United States. In response, a group of U.S. women formed their own group called MADRE whose purpose, according to Executive Director Kathy Engel, was "to get women here to connect the issues they face in their own communities with the effect of our policies in Central America."

Sarandon joined MADRE as one of its founding members and, emboldened by her growing knowledge and passion, was now quite ready to talk about Central American issues. With the by now cult status of *The Rocky Horror Picture Show* and the critical success of *Pretty Baby* and *Atlantic City*, Sarandon was beginning to find herself in demand as a speaker on college campuses. Sarandon assumed that talking to students in the eighties would not be that different from the Free Speech Movement at Berkeley in the sixties and that, after the expected shop talk about her film and theater career, she would engage the students in a spirited dialogue about political and social issues.

As typified by a 1983 appearance at Harvard University, what she often found was a frustrating lack of knowledge or interest on the part of students. "I tried to talk about Central America and the students were saying, 'It's not our problem, it doesn't concern us. We can't be interested in this rinky-dink country.' They reminded me of people of my parent's generation, the post-Depression attitude."

Sarandon would become more combative at subsequent campus visits, openly challenging students to examine issues and, above all, to care. "At one point you have to decide to stand up and be counted," she said at an early 1984 lecture at UCLA.

Shortly after the UCLA speech, MADRE announced that members of their group would be traveling to Nicaragua to bring baby food and milk to struggling families. Sarandon was invited to go along.

"I decided to make the trip with MADRE to Nicaragua to do something practical; to take milk and baby food to women who needed it. This trip also seemed a perfect way to meet people and to try to understand what's going on there, while also accomplishing something specific. I believe in practicality."

And it was that practicality that gave her pause to reflect on what going to Nicaragua might do to her career. She admitted to fearing being branded with the "Communist" or "Hanoi Jane" tag. But her personal commitment was so strong that Sarandon also feared the impact of not really seeing the truth.

Sarandon was not going to Nicaragua under the official

auspices of the U.S. government and she was not going as part of a star-studded celebrity group. There would be no photo ops or media coverage and, given what she knew about the situation in Nicaragua, she could find herself in danger. More than one person suggested that the actress not go. Sarandon was very much on her own in this adventure and felt the cause was just. And so, as she packed her bags, she felt she was doing the right thing.

What Sarandon and the other members of MADRE would see during their eight days in Nicaragua was eye opening. They walked through bombed-out daycare centers, witnessed children playing in abandoned tanks, and saw young children begging for pencils rather than money.

Sarandon saw things she was not prepared to see. In every small town they passed through, Sarandon and the members of MADRE would hear tales from the village women about the children they had lost to the Contras and the atrocities that had been perpetrated on them and their people in the name of freedom. But always at the end of these stories would be the believable and heartfelt determination to continue to fight the revolution for freedom, even if it cost them their lives.

Sarandon's trip to Nicaragua came at a physical cost when she came down with typhoid. But that did not stop her from being enveloped by passion for the cause.

In the end Sarandon came back to the States more committed than ever to fighting against Contra funding.

Sarandon returned to the United States just as Congress was getting ready for another vote on Contra aid. In the past, the vote had been a fairly rote, rubber-stamp formality with little in the way of opposition being voiced. But Sarandon, as well as other members of the growing anti-Contra forces in the United States, were much in evidence at the 1984 congressional meetings.

Sarandon was quiet but passionate as she sat before the congressional committee comprised of old white men, patently informing them of the things she had seen and heard in Nicaragua and the cold, hard financial facts that while the United States was sending upward of $400 million a year to Nicaragua and neighboring countries to fund questionable government policies, an estimated 100,000 U.S. children were living on the streets.

In the end, Congress voted to continue to support the Contras but it was not the across-the-board support that had been the norm in previous sessions and a lot more questions were beginning to be asked. Sarandon looked at her presence in Congress as a moral victory in which she got to make some points and call some heretofore unknown realities about America's involvement in Central America to the public's attention.

The media was suddenly all over the Nicaraguan issue, due in large part to the publicity generated by the MADRE trip and by Sarandon's high-profile presence at the Contra funding hearings. And Sarandon, for the first time solely in the celebrity spotlight for her activist work, engaged the press in spirited dialogues in which she impressed the often-cynical media by actually knowing what she was talking about and explaining it in a straightforward, concise manner.

Unfortunately, the resultant coverage was not always kind. While women's magazines like *Vogue* and liberal outlets such as the *Progressive* would ultimately treat the issue and Sarandon with respect, many mainstream pop-culture outlets like *People* were eager to jump on the easy target of Sarandon as the eighties' answer to Jane Fonda, quickly dismissing her and her efforts as the work of "Hanoi Susan."

As it turned out, the U.S. government did not take kindly to Sarandon's activism and growing presence in a number of movements and causes.

Shortly after appearing before Congress, the actress found herself being tagged as "a supporter of international terrorism" by both the FBI and the CIA. Sarandon, in a *Time Out* conversation, took her promotion to political enemy of the state as a badge of honor.

"I suppose they did not want Americans telling anyone what was happening there, because, at that point, nobody really knew where Nicaragua was, let alone what our tax dollars were doing."

Her growing presence as an activist to be reckoned with reached its apex during that period when Sarandon was notified by the American Civil Liberties Union (ACLU) that she had been targeted by an extreme right-wing group called Western Goals for what they considered "un-American" and "Communist" activities. She was proud of the fact that she was in great company because Western Goals had also targeted the likes of Joan Baez, Richard Dreyfuss, and Studs Terkel on the same list.

The early days of the Reagan administration had begun to cast a giant shadow on the land. The rise of the religious right and its collective attitude of being uncomfortable with certain kinds of expression was beginning to make headway in the decidedly conservative White House and the beginning of inroads into the freedoms set forth by the Constitution. Rather than closing their eyes to what they deemed offensive, a growing number of powerful political groups were proclaiming that there were certain things that nobody should see.

And one of the first things they set their sights on was art. What particularly bothered these groups were works of art that had gay or sexually explicit themes or what they considered sacrilegious themes. The leaders of these organizations knew that, under the First Amendment, they could not directly censor these things. So they attempted to exert influence on politicians to force the National Endowment for the Arts (NEA) to cut off funding by threatening new and even more restrictive pressure on the organization.

In response to this threat of censorship raining down from the White House, a group of actors who lived in New York formed a group called the Creative Coalition to attempt to counteract the attacks on the NEA. Susan Sarandon was among the founding members.

Ira Glasser, executive director of the ACLU, recalls that his organization was heavily involved with the resistance and litigation against the anti-art movement. Glasser recalled that part of his job entailed his appearance at early meetings of the Creative Coalition and it was there that he met Susan Sarandon and other celebrities who wanted to know what they could do and how to do it.

"One of the things they wanted to do was to organize themselves to go testify before Congress on this issue because Congress was holding hearings," recalled Glasser. "Actors come to these issues with a lot of public visibility and everyone automatically assumes they're experts. But what they know, they know as citizens and everyone thinks they're experts. When the reality is that most are hardly in the position to be experts and most have no experience testifying, much less know the law, the politics and the issues."

But when a number of Creative Coalition members, including Susan, decided they wanted to testify before Congress, Glasser agreed to be a mentor and brief them on both the content of the law and what testifying in Congress would be like. Susan agreed to meet with Glasser in his office.

On the appointed date, Sarandon, dressed simply in blue jeans and flannel shirt, her hair done up in a conservative bun, took a cab across town to meet with Glasser. The ACLU director remembered that day.

"I would have been willing to meet her anywhere because a lot of people in the public limelight do not like to be walking around. But Susan wasn't like that. She said she'd just come up. She looked gorgeous when she walked in, but not the way you'd expect to see her in public. She was just being very ordinary and unassuming. She was totally unpretentious. Susan had mastered the art of being unaware of who she was. She just came in, walked up to the receptionist, and announced herself. The people working in the office were a little bit dazzled."

Susan walked into Glasser's office. For the next hour, Glasser briefed her on what she could expect from a congressional testimony and how best to get her point across and how to respond to the questions that would come from the congressmen. Glasser recalled that he was essentially giving Susan all the necessary background information and then letting her write her own script. And he found her to be an apt pupil.

"It was total serious business," recalled Glasser. "There was no star stuff, no chitchat. She was coming there for a serious purpose and we just got right to it. Susan approached it all quite seriously. She did her homework. She asked intelligent questions. She knew what she knew. She knew what she did not know. And she knew what she needed to find out."

By design, the ACLU was not present at the hearings, preferring to let the actors do their own thing without the impression of being mere puppets of the ACLU. Glasser reflected, "The whole idea was to have them talk in their own terms, to know what the law was. Susan was used to being in the public eye and was completely comfortable. What I was worried about was that she would not be thrown by being in the Senate chambers. From what I heard, the hearings went very well."

So well, in fact, that potentially damaging legislation did not get passed and the NEA wound up issuing rules that were a lot less restrictive than they could have been under congressional edicts. "The whole issue was contained," said Glasser, "and part of the reason for that was that people like Susan were willing to come forward and up the ante a little bit."

Sarandon turned her attention from the arts to nuclear proliferation in June of 1983 when she was one of the driving forces behind a massive antinuclear rally in New York's Central Park. During a fiery speech at the rally, she pointed out her distrust of the Russians, President Ronald Reagan, and anybody who had access to an important button.

Predictably, Sarandon took a beating from a number of sources for what many considered her un-American platform. "This isn't about capitalism or communism," she told a *Cosmopolitan* reporter. "If the bombs drop, there won't be any isms to fret about. This is about life and safety."

Sarandon's activism during this period was not limited to just national issues. Now very aware of the often contrary ways in which U.S. taxpayer money is spent by state and federal government, the actress was quick to support national and even local issues. Late in 1984, Sarandon traveled to Los Angeles where, along with fellow actors Mike Farrell and Richard Dreyfuss, she joined a class-action lawsuit being brought against the Los Angeles Police Department and its chief, Daryl Gates, charging that taxpayer funds were being spent to defend the department against alleged illegal spying lawsuits that had been filed against the police.

What was obvious during the early years of the eighties

was Sarandon's growing political and social awareness that saw her stepping more frequently into the activist arena. But what is usually overlooked is that, collectively, the years 1980–84 were a rarely acknowledged watershed of good work. *Atlantic City* and, to a lesser degree, *Tempest* were sit-up-and-take-notice kinds of performances. But easily Sarandon's bravest choices were in the theater where *White Chicks* and *Extremities* saw the actress coming to grips with her true potential. Sarandon continued to make some questionable choices in such entertaining but ultimately doomed efforts like *The Hunger* and *The Buddy System*. She was continuing to fly in the face of Hollywood stereotyping with a series of offbeat, challenging choices.

Throughout 1984, Sarandon worked sporadically; primarily in small roles in television miniseries as *A.D. Anno Domini* and *Mussolini & I*. The roles were largely forgettable compared to the real-life drama being played out in Sarandon's life.

Franco Amurri was an Italian director of some notoriety in Europe and a man possessed of earthy good looks and charisma. When Sarandon met him, she immediately fell under his spell. As with all of her previous relationships, it was hard to separate the love from the lust in their affair, which meant, in Sarandon's case, the odds were good that it would not last long. Only one thing complicated this situation.

Late in 1984 Sarandon, after being told in no uncertain terms that she could not have children, found herself preg-

113

nant. "After I contracted typhoid, I went to Italy and miraculouly became pregnant. I think it (the disease) burned something. A kind of purification ritual was imposed on me through typhoid. I thought, This little soul really wants to be here, so it's meant to be."

When she informed Amurri that he was about to be a father, the director mouthed all the right platitudes about being there for her and the child. But marriage, if it was discussed at all, was never a serious option for either of them. They agreed that Amurri would be a part of his child's life and that there would be reasonable visitation.

But neither was blind to the reality that this was going to be a difficult situation and that they would have to be civilized in handling it. And it was to their credit that, in the ensuing years, their child never heard a harsh word uttered about either parent and, when they were in each other's company, Sarandon and Amurri were always warm and affectionate to each other in their child's presence.

Eventually Amurri returned to Italy and the formal relationship ended, leaving Sarandon in New York dealing with the onset of motherhood as an unmarried woman.

Sarandon recalled that she was determined to go ahead with having the child and told Amurri in no uncertain terms that she would go through the birth with or without his participation. "It was pretty loose," she told *Playboy*. "Was I ever frightened about doing it alone? I think probably no."

Sarandon's long-held beliefs regarding marriage and relationships did not preclude her being an unwed mother.

And it was not likely that her career, unlike that of actress Ingrid Bergman years earlier, was going to be adversely affected by this now relatively trendy practice. But there was a degree of discomfort at the prospect of breaking the news to her parents, centered around her Catholic upbringing and the associated guilt.

"The baby was probably pretty shocking (to them)," she recalled in *Mother Jones*. "When I told my father I was pregnant he said he thought it was something I'd probably always wanted and he was happy for me and that's the only thing he's ever said. I really don't know what they feel about it. And obviously they're not comfortable discussing it."

Sarandon's pregnancy forced her to make yet another life decision. Unbeknownst to even her closest friends, Sarandon's increased involvement in political and social activism was having a spiritual and emotional effect on her. So much so that she was seriously considering giving up acting.

She told the *Los Angeles Times*, "If my daughter hadn't been given to me as a gift, I'd probably have gone further and further into political work because I was definitely at a point where I was looking to do something that made a difference."

In the face of this change in her life, Sarandon remained pragmatic. She realized that she probably had enough time to squeeze in one more film role before it would be time to deliver, and that she would not be working for a period of time after the birth. And so, once again not so much interested in quality as availability, she grabbed onto the film *Compromising Positions*, a slight

115

and ultimately uneven melding of a murder mystery and black comedy in which Sarandon played the role of the wife of a murdered philandering dentist who attempts to find his killer.

The script had a lot working against it from the outset, largely expository and a whodunit in which the audience tended to know the answers before the questions were asked. Sarandon sensed that she had been hired because she was up to the task of laying out the exposition and that scant attention would be paid to refining or guiding her character. Consequently, for much of the shoot, Sarandon was faced with just trying to find something to make each scene work for her.

Sarandon sensed that *Compromising Positions* would not be a work of art. But she consoled herself with the fact that "It paid for my first child."

chapter five
"THE LONELINESS OF THAT PERIOD WAS HORRIBLE"

Expectant motherhood was tough on Susan Sarandon. She could not in her wildest dreams have
imagined the horrors of morning sickness and swollen
ankles to be worse than what she was experiencing. There
were also the moments when the reality that she was
about to become a single mother hit her hard. Logically
she felt she could handle her situation. Emotionally she
was all over the map.

But given these physical and emotional obstacles, the
pregnancy was fairly easy. Franco Amurri was in the picture and would be there for the birth of his and Sarandon's
child.

Eva Marie Livia Amurri was born midway through
1985. Sarandon, all enigmatic and somewhat self-cen-
tered, was emotional and teary-eyed as she breast-fed her
daughter for the first time. Sarandon was delighted at the
prospect of motherhood and, despite her anticonventional
attitudes, was, by all accounts, the traditional mother in a
very nontraditional situation.

To what degree the birth of Eva succeeded in mending fences between Sarandon and her parents is not clear. Their ongoing dissatisfaction with the way their daughter had chosen to live her life was apparent. One can only speculate that Lenora, given her history, was taking Sarandon's single motherhood particularly hard. In a perfect world, Phillip and Lenora would have been at their daughter's side. But Sarandon's world was anything but perfect and, like almost everything connected to her relationship with her parents, Sarandon has never talked about it.

The necessity of taking time off from a relatively glamorous and always interesting life to be a mother also gave her time to reflect on where she was at this point in her life. Her personal choices had led her to being a thirty-nine-year-old, single mother and, not too surprisingly, she was comfortable with that. There was no sadness in the fact that there was no significant other in her life. And she did not look back on her past relationships with an overriding sense of loss. She would have no trouble living with the decisions she had made.

Her professional life was another matter.

Sarandon, who was approaching forty, had had an interesting yet erratic career to that point but not one that had translated into an A-list actress despite the critical successes of *Pretty Baby* and *Atlantic City*. Academy award nomination aside, the reality was that she was still nothing more than a struggling actress who, with her choices, had not been able to capitalize fully on her talents. And with the arrival of Eva, Sarandon was convinced that her stock would most certainly plummet even further during her hiatus from acting and, while comfortable with the decision, worried that she would have trouble supporting herself and her daughter.

She began to entertain other job options. Her activism had opened a lot of doors that might lead to what she felt would be more rewarding albeit less lucrative work. She entertained the thought of teaching. But on a very conscious level, the immediate future looked bleak.

"I was feeling particularly useless, sinking into too much self-obsession. And I thought, Oh I'll go and read fairy tales to little children in beds somewhere."

Said partly in jest, Sarandon began to take the notion of doing some street-level volunteer work seriously and began making inquiries at area hospitals. Eventually she discovered a program at Mount Sinai Hospital that appeared to be right up her alley. At the time, Mount Sinai conducted what many considered a cutting-edge therapy program called Theatre Games for its schizophrenic patients in which the elements of art, music, and play-acting were combined to encourage patients to interact with people around them and, by association, the outside world.

Sarandon would become a major participant in the Theatre Games program, showing up every Tuesday and Thursday, with Eva in tow, often staying from early morning to late at night, to work with the patients. The therapy offered by Theatre Games worked both ways and Sarandon found herself lifted out of her depression by the

119

interaction with the patients and the knowledge that she was contributing something to the welfare of others.

That Sarandon could find inner strength and a sense of therapy in her own good works was not unusual. Helping others had always come naturally to her but now, perhaps on a subconscious level, she was finding it an effective way to beat the blues and, most importantly, to put her life in emotional balance. Not that Sarandon did not love her life. It was just that she was getting a bit restless.

As Sarandon would discover, motherhood was a full-time job and she remained emotionally invested in bringing up her daughter. But as the months went by, and Sarandon became secure in the fact that she could be a working mother and her daughter would indeed not suffer, the actress began thinking about returning to work.

Her first step on the road back was the role of Colonel Margaret Ann Jessup in the 1986 television film *Women of Valor*. This tale of World War II nurses struggling to survive the horrors of a Japanese prison camp had a surreal and dated feel to it that ultimately doomed the film to run-of-the-mill stature. But it had been a good working experience, one that allowed Sarandon to shake off the rust, regain her confidence, and reenter the working world.

What she discovered as she attempted to get back to acting was that her worst fears had become a reality. What had turned into a nearly eighteen-month break had greatly diminished her status in Hollywood. She was now being told that she would have to audition for even the most inconsequential roles. Sarandon did not like it and, truth be known, often felt humiliated and degraded at the prospect of having to audition at this point in her career.

But, with her survivor's instinct firmly in place, Sarandon would go dutifully before the producers and grovel. Often the things she was auditioning for were rubbish and she knew it. But she could likewise sense when something was worth fighting for.

And the role in *The Witches of Eastwick* was definitely an opportunity in the making.

The Witches of Eastwick was big-time Hollywood—an A-list cast that included Jack Nicholson and Michelle Pfeiffer and a skilled director in George Miller in what was reportedly a sexy-supernatural comedy. It seemed overtly mainstream and commercial and that was something Sarandon needed at the moment.

The Witches of Eastwick, based on the John Updike novel, chronicled the sexual awakening of three lonely New England women after they come in contact with the mysterious Mephisto Miller. The script was raucous and wildly funny and, for Sarandon, it would be a high-profile reentry. Sarandon aggressively pursued and ultimately captured the pivotal role of Alex, the ringleader of the three title characters. Because the ironing out of contract particulars was often a painstaking, laborious job of crossing t's and dotting i's, Sarandon was not too concerned that she did not have anything specific in writing when she reported to the set for rehearsals.

She should have been . . .

A mere four days before rehearsals were set to begin,

Sarandon was informed that she had been replaced in the role by Cher and offered what Sarandon would later describe as the "nonexistent" role of the repressed cello player, Jane. Her new character literally had one scene in the beginning and then disappeared for the remainder of the film.

What followed was an angry bout of accusations, threats, and all-around bad blood between Sarandon and the producers of the film. Admittedly this was not Cher's fault. The pop-singer-turned-actress was hot on the strength of her performances in *Silkwood* and *Mask* and word of mouth was excellent on the just-completed *Moonstruck*. Sarandon understood that reality and did not have any animosity toward her. Sarandon immediately saw her director, George Miller, as the bad guy in this drama. In the months following the completion of the film she would accuse him of being the type of director who put the good of the film ahead of the feelings of his actors.

Motherhood had not dampened Sarandon's sense of right and wrong. Instinctively she knew she had to make a stand.

Sarandon threatened to walk off the film. But the studio quickly pointed out that she was contractually bound to do the movie. Sarandon once again felt backed into a corner.

"The loneliness of that period was horrible," she told the *New York Daily News*.

"I was pretty much a single mom at that point, and I could have fought it in court, but I didn't have any money and the studio's lawyers could have prevented me from working elsewhere if I walked away."

The responsibility of motherhood weighed heavily on Sarandon during those dark days when she contemplated walking off *Witches of Eastwick*. There was real concern and a bit of self-loathing as she contemplated returning to the film and a greatly reduced role.

Against her better judgment, Sarandon agreed to go with her minuscule role in *Witches*. Perhaps feeling guilty, the producers had the script hastily rewritten in a half-hearted attempt to give some substance to Sarandon's character while the actress, in the spirit of cooperation, took some impromptu cello lessons to add some sense of realism to basically what was a nondescript character. Sarandon was feeling betrayed and, no doubt, more than a little like a submissive little girl for knuckling under to the studio but decided to turn that to her advantage.

Admittedly the challenge of making something out of an almost nonexistent character was not going to be easy. On paper, the part was little more than a shadow of a char- acter, with no discerning substance. And so, as the pro- ducers made a halfhearted attempt to rewrite the script to accommodate her, Sarandon chose to simply ignore the script and do what she wanted to do.

Which meant a largely improvisational approach to the role in which Sarandon exploited the fact that her char- acter was so insignificant that nobody could say for sure if what she was doing in front of the camera was right or wrong. "Since there was no through line we could agree on, no through line for my character, my way of dealing with that was to never read the script. I just tried to come up with ideas for each scene to make things work."

All of which made the actress's time on the set much more enjoyable than she could have imagined. She got to be good friends with costar Jack Nicholson. And although she was nearly electrocuted in the scene in which her character levitates over a swimming pool, she came out of what she termed "an amusing, horrible situation" with a modicum of satisfaction.

But not without learning some tough lessons about herself and the film business. Sarandon, in looking back on her *Witches of Eastwick* experience, recalled that she went "from sobbing and feeling humiliated" to finding a way to "sever whatever ego involvement was there."

She also reveled in the irony that she learned a lot from doing that film that she would probably never have to use again unless she changed jobs and became a gun runner.

"I learned that a promise is not a promise," she told the *Chicago Tribune*, "and a person's word is not a person's word."

Sarandon in the troughs of cynicism is not a pretty sight. What comes out are detached, almost matter-of-fact pronouncements that are cold in their logic and leave little in the way of maneuvering room. But ultimately it became a defense mechanism that worked for her.

And it was in full bloom during the round of press interviews for *Witches*. Sarandon's part in the film had been so small that there was a question about whether it was worthwhile having her do any press. And the producers were well aware that the actress could be a loose cannon. They agreed, however, that Sarandon did have some name recognition, and so they crossed their fingers.

In the past, Sarandon had not been shy about voicing her displeasure at a bad filmmaking experience but, in the aftermath of *Witches*, she was close to vicious in attacks that often began and ended with the horrors of the film industry and offered cynical proclamations on the deteriorating state of the U.S. government.

During interviews essentially designed to promote the film, she lashed out at the process by which the United States chose its leaders, admonishing reporters that Americans elected their leaders based on personality rather than ability and then sat back as the politicians made their choices for them.

Studio executives were obviously cringing at the idea of Sarandon on her soapbox. But they kept her out on the stump for *The Witches of Eastwick* and Sarandon kept on attacking.

"I think they [studio executives] encourage people to be difficult," she said in a classic case of biting the hand that feeds her. "I think we may be at a low point in terms of integrity, honesty, self-respect and obviously they're very patronizing toward the movie audience."

Sarandon's candor only succeeded in adding to the already lengthy antiestablishment traits that, by age forty, had made the actress persona non grata in much of Hollywood. For Sarandon was too old at this point to believably play anything but her age or a little younger and those few age-specific roles that were available were being gobbled up by the likes of Meryl Streep, Jane Fonda, and a select few over-forty actresses. Her erratic choices had made even typecasting her next to impossible.

"Not only was I not on the A list," she said. "I wasn't on any list at all."

What she was also discovering was that, in a twisted sort of Hollywood way, she had gotten to a point in her life where she felt she was overqualified for the parts she was getting. "I was always called in to make something more of a part that was lacking in at least two dimensions. I'd been in a lot of situations that weren't particularly respectful and where I wasn't treated very well."

No one would have blamed the actress if, with *The Witches of Eastwick* being the proverbial last straw, she had decided to give up acting and try another career. Those close to Sarandon sensed, as she did, that her growing prowess in the activist arena and her natural instincts for teaching would have put her in line for a number of jobs. But while she was not ready to give up on a career she had invested twenty years of her life in, she was admittedly at a loss as to what to do next.

Sarandon decided that rather than stay in New York and feel sorry for the lack of career advancement, she would go to Europe for an extended vacation that included a stopover in Italy to visit with her daughter's father. While in Italy, Sarandon received a copy of a script by a relatively unknown screenwriter and budding director named Ron Shelton entitled *Bull Durham*. Cynically, she assumed it was another castoff that nobody else wanted. But her attitude changed once she read the script.

The story, involving an aging baseball catcher, a young pitcher, and a literature professor-baseball groupie named Annie Savoy, transcended the typical baseball comedy. Sarandon thought the story was a sweet and poignant ode to following one's dream. The script also appealed to her idea of debunking the myths of sexuality and the true costs of failure and of making money. Annie Savoy was also that rare, unpredictable screen character whose final denouement was in doubt until the very end.

Sarandon wanted the part very badly. It was a breakout role in the making and, realistically, she was a working actress who needed a part this good to elevate her dormant status in the industry. Realistically she knew that there was a lot working against her landing it.

Orion Pictures, the studio producing *Bull Durham*, was not particularly interested in having Sarandon read for the role and had already drawn up a short list, which reportedly included Michelle Pfeiffer, of those they considered the more bankable actresses in town. However, Annie Savoy was proving a difficult character to cast. The very unorthodox nature of the character scared many actresses off. Director-writer Shelton rejected others. That Shelton insisted all actors read for the part put off still others.

At this point, Sarandon had no problem "groveling"

and "kissing ass" in order to get the part. And so, through persistence, she managed to get the studio heads and Shelton to agree to meet with her. Sarandon had to pay for the flight from Italy to Los Angeles out of her own pocket which, at the time, was money she did not have to spend. On the flight back to Los Angeles, she played out all the possible scenarios in her head, including the one where she would walk away without the role.

Sarandon would later recall that she played the Hollywood game real well; meeting with and "kissing the ass" of Kevin Costner who was starring in *Bull Durham* convinced Shelton that she could handle Annie's diversified character and she finally won the approval of the studio executives by appearing at her interview with them in a tight-fitting dress. When she set her mind to it, Sarandon proved she could play the game she so despised and walked away with the part of Annie Savoy.

She would later discover that in playing up to Kevin Costner she had made the right decision because, except for the script, Orion was not happy with Shelton, Sarandon, or any of the other actors and that it was only Costner's obvious clout and his insistence that the studio go with his and Shelton's choices that got the part for Sarandon.

Luck was definitely riding with Sarandon on *Bull Durham*. In a town rife with egos, it's all too easy to rub somebody the wrong way. Where Sarandon would have gone, careerwise, if she had not gotten *Bull Durham* is anybody's guess. Chances are she would have continued

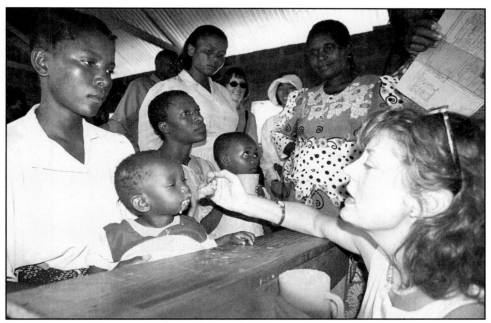

UNICEF Goodwill Ambassador Susan Sarandon feeds a young child during a 2000 visit to a healthcare community center in Mwanza, Tanzania. *(Antony Njuguna/Reuters/Archives Photo)*

Susan Sarandon learned about the secondary horror of AIDS during a visit to Tanzania when she discovered that many children were orphaned by the AIDS-related death of their parents. *(Antony Njuguna/Reuters/Archives Photos)*

Susan Sarandon (holding T-shirt), Paul Newman (second from left), Richard Dreyfuss (bottom left), Marisa Tomei (left), and John Leguizamo (bottom right) marched in support of striking commercial actors during a rally in Manhattan in September 2000. (*Mike Segar/Reuters/Archives Photos*)

Susan Sarandon and Tim Robbins march with other actors in support of the five-month-long strike by the Screen Actors Guild. The work stoppage brought the commercial industry to a standstill in 2000. (*Mike Segar/Reuters/Archives Photos*)

Sarandon broke a personal Oscar drought when she received Best Actress honors for *Dead Man Walking* at the 1996 Academy Awards ceremony. (*Barry King/Getty Images*)

Susan Sarandon walks down the red carpet at the 1997 Academy Awards ceremony. (*Ron Wolfson/Getty Images*)

Linking hands with local politicians and activists, Sarandon marched in protest of police brutality in New York City during a 1999 rally. *(Porter Gifford/Getty Images)*

Sarandon and members of the Center for Constitutional Rights block the entrance to Police Plaza during a 1999 demonstration to protest the shooting of West African immigrant Amadou Diallo. *(Richard B. Levine/Getty Images)*

Susan Sarandon, backed by actor James Naughton, states her case for striking actors on Capitol Hill during a congressional briefing in October 2000. (*Carucha Meuse/Reuters/Archives Photos*)

Sarandon took the time to play with children at the Ashray Home in Mumbai, India, during a UNICEF-sponsored visit to see firsthand the ravages of AIDS on families. (*Roger Lemoyne/Getty Images*)

to slug it out in the kind of films that paid the bills and perhaps she would have eventually hit another *Bull Durham*.

Fortunately, in Costner she came up against somebody who appreciated her straightforward, no-nonsense approach. Costner could not have not known he was being schmoozed. But he was able to look past the smoke screen and see Sarandon for who she was—a very talented actress.

Sarandon would later recall that making *Bull Durham* was a difficult working experience because there was not a lot of time or money involved. But those things were more than balanced out by the fact that *Bull Durham*, under the guidance of first-time director Shelton, was transformed into an ongoing, supportive community in which actors were the recipients of a respectful, collaborative environment. Much of this attitude came from Shelton whose raw rookie status translated into an easygoing feeling on the set. And it was the director who felt that Sarandon definitely made the role of Annie Savoy come alive.

"Annie could have easily been played as a flake," Shelton said in an *American Film* interview. "Susan brought experience and commitment, substance and dignity to the part. Also it was my first film as a director and she put me at ease in a wonderful way. The first week of filming, she said, 'Look, I never went to film school. Just say, "Louder, softer, faster, slower." ' It cut the mystique right out."

And, in the process, what made for a magical meeting

of actor and role. Sarandon enthusiastically claimed at the time that Annie Savoy was one of the best women's roles she had encountered. She saw Annie as a woman of many facets: sexy, uninhibited, vulnerable, and a total free spirit.

Within the good old boy atmosphere that permeated the movie, Sarandon's Annie Savoy was truly the center of the universe. Whether it was in dealing with the realities of Costner's character on the downside of his career and the consequence of failure or leading the Robbins character through the emotional minefield of manhood and success, Sarandon exuded a masterful control of her character.

As if the role was not enough of a victory, it was also on the set of *Bull Durham* that Sarandon discovered her soul mate in the guise of costar Tim Robbins. "My daughter chose him before I did. When we were making the movie, I was always having these big barbecues and Kevin [Costner] and the guys from the team would come. Eva would always gravitate toward Tim and he was great with her."

For Sarandon, Robbins was literally a mirror image. His career had, likewise, been marked by quirky choices that included *Five Corners*, *Made in Heaven,* and *Toy Soldiers*. He was a politically and socially aware individual who was not afraid to make his opinion known. He was not somebody that Sarandon instinctively felt she would have to baby and boss around. She felt his creative energy and passion. And, much like Chris Sarandon and Louis Malle, there was a sense of individuality and self-confidence that was equally as attractive as his rugged, still boyish good looks. There was only one potential obstacle to anything beyond an on-set friendship.

Tim Robbins was twelve years younger than Susan Sarandon.

Age had never been a consideration for Sarandon who, in many of her previous relationships, had been a dozen years or more younger than her men. She looked on the age difference being reversed as just part of the karma that surrounded her life. Robbins did not seem to care either.

Sarandon knew instantly that there was chemistry between them.

"When a person sees another person, really sees another person, that for me is where the sexual tension comes from," she said in a *Milwaukee Journal Sentinel* interview. "This feeling that a person really sees you, maybe accepts you and you go from there."

Likewise, Robbins recalled Sarandon in somewhat existential terms. He admired her spirit and attitude. She was somebody with whom he could have a serious discussion and turn right around and share a dirty joke. But he would often recall in later years that what had initially attracted him to the actress was that she was smart as well as beautiful.

Robbins, who had remained emotionally on an even keel in previous relationships, was head over heels smitten. Robbins's brother David recalled in a *GQ* article receiving a telephone call from Robbins not long after filming commenced on *Bull Durham*. "He seemed like a teenager. I had never heard him like that."

In a matter of weeks, the costars quite naturally moved their relationship along and became lovers. They seemed a perfect match in their physical and intellectual desires.

131

But, from the beginning, there was some question whether the relationship would endure. Sarandon's recent visit with Amurri had rekindled some old feelings and there was some question about whether Sarandon would return to him. But while the filming of *Bull Durham* continued, the least-kept secret on the set was that Robbins and Sarandon were an item.

Shortly after completion of the film, Sarandon and Robbins went their separate ways. Both had questions about where the relationship was going and felt some time apart was necessary. Sarandon surmised that she had just had the latest in a series of on-set romances and that it was now over.

After the filming of *Bull Durham* ended, Sarandon split from Amurri in February. At the end of August, Sarandon discovered that she was once again pregnant. She was concerned that this would be Amurri redux and that she would again be plunged into the turmoil of single motherhood. Sarandon had no idea how Robbins would react to the news. Admittedly he was stunned. But once he got over the surprise, Robbins made it clear that he was there for her and that their relationship had, for him, turned to love.

The couple agreed to move in together—another surprise for Sarandon. And while there was no talk of marriage, the relationship, in their minds, was already permanent.

"It's not like we're making any political kind of statement," Robbins reflected in *US*. "I feel like I am married to her. We have made a long-term commitment to each other. So nothing beyond that is necessary."

Perhaps not for Robbins. But for Sarandon, setting up house with the actor was entering uncharted territory.

With the exception of her traditional marriage to Chris, Sarandon had always found herself in nontraditional relationships. She once matter-of-factly talked about living with a man (whom she refused to identify) who had two children by two different women and that they all got together for the holidays. There had been the romance with Amurri that had produced Eva and found her a willing single mother.

But now, having a child with a man who was forthright in his willingness to take responsibility? That was forcing her to become part of a family. And the idea of doing that and actually making it work was more frightening to her than anything that had challenged her in her life. But the fact that Tim seemed to Sarandon to be sane, open-minded, and undamaged led her to believe that this relationship might just work.

Once again flying in the face of conventional Hollywood wisdom, Sarandon took eighteen months off to have her and Robbins's first child, a boy named Jack Henry Robbins. Rather appropriately, Sarandon's first child with Robbins was christened by the Reverend Jesse Jackson during a homeless march in which the new parents participated. Although her absence effectively stopped cold the momentum she was building on the good word of mouth about her performance in *Bull Durham*, Sarandon was quite content to sit back and enjoy motherhood.

But she was not unaware that the accolades were continuing to pour in for her performance in *Bull Durham*. The *New York Times* announced, "She looks terrific and possesses the sort of comic authority one usually recognizes on the stage. She takes control of the film." The *Los Angeles Times* took the damned-with-faint-praise approach when it offered, "For all the tough-soft dimension that Sarandon gives her, Annie is really a paper-thin vehicle for a man's warmest imaginings." *Newsweek* praised her, "Sarandon is so irresistible in the part it may not strike you until afterward that she's a total male fantasy figure." The *Village Voice* played on that theme by saying, "There's no choice but to be hypnotized. She's the classic American flake."

Sarandon would joke with friends and in press interviews that 1988 could be the year that she became a major star. But the buzz was tempered for Sarandon by eighteen years in the filmmaking business and all the previous perceived "disappointments" and "heartaches" that had succeeded in damping down the glamour. Sure the reviews were nice but Sarandon was just grateful to be considered a working actress. But she would be lying if she said that *Bull Durham* did not whet her appetite for stardom.

However, she did concede that *Bull Durham* did change her attitude about the industry and her place in it.

She was becoming increasingly disillusioned with being an actress because she felt that as a woman she was not being treated with respect by the industry. Her growing disillusionment with the process and the system had much to do with the impression that she was working with mediocre talents who had limited ambitions and who lacked passion for the work. She reasoned that her involvement in past projects had a lot to do with her trying to make more of a film than was actually there. But she felt that the success of *Bull Durham* had resurrected her career and restored her faith in herself.

The reality was that a combination of motherhood, a solid relationship with Robbins, and the full-blown success of *Bull Durham* had finally succeeded in sharpening the actress's attitude to a fine point. Whereas in the past she would tend to gloss over weaknesses in projects if her role was good, she was now inspired to look at the big picture. Sarandon, past forty, had finally grown up.

Before *Bull Durham* Sarandon, perhaps tiring of the mundane but thoroughly enjoyable life of motherhood, agreed to step back into her career to portray the role of an older, uneducated waitress who falls in love with a young, widowed lawyer in the film *White Palace*.

Sarandon had to chuckle when she heard the story line. She seemed almost too perfect for the role for obvious reasons. And it is to her credit that the actress saw past the gimmicky nature of the story and saw the elegance and reality in the source material, the novel by Glenn Savan.

Sarandon was so determined to make the middle-aged Nora a flesh-and-blood character that she willingly agreed to put on fifteen pounds of extra weight to give her character more credibility as the greasy-spoon charmer. But *White Palace*, in which James Spader was ultimately cast

135

as her younger lover, took a long time to develop. In the meantime, Sarandon's interest waned as the joys of motherhood began to take up more and more of her time and thoughts. By the time Sarandon arrived at the St. Louis location for *White Palace*, the actress was short on enthusiasm.

She was nursing her baby at the time and feeling more like a mother than an actress. The outlook for anything about *White Palace* rekindling her enthusiasm and interest seemed doubtful.

As always, the work itself proved the cure for any doubts Sarandon was having. The script had, given the creative license often employed in Hollywood, remained surprisingly loyal to the source material. The tone, despite the potential for soap opera, rang true with crisp dialogue and a realistic sense of time and place. Director Luis Mandoki seemed sensitive to the story's subtle, less obvious moments and was more than willing to give his actors room to fully explore their characters. And whether on a subconscious level or not, Sarandon seemed to reflect a lot in her past relationships in her scenes with Spader. Their chemistry showed up in a wide range of emotions and, most important, in a believable tale of unconventional love.

White Palace also turned out to be a challenge on a personal front. Despite her sexually charged image on screen, Sarandon had, to that point, avoided doing anything approaching a protracted nude scene which *White Palace* required. Sarandon was comfortable with her body but was adamant that the scene play as real, rather than gratuitous and exploitive. When it came to that sequence, her only criterion had been met. That it was integral to the story and the development of the relationship of the characters was a good enough reason. By the time principal photography had been completed, Sarandon saw *White Palace* as a courageous act.

"Two misfits taking the chance to reach out to each other," she explained. "For me that's a very political act."

Hollywood, chaffing at the early presidential candidates in 1990 taking easy and inevitable shots at movie sex and violence, chose *White Palace* to show Washington that they were trying to clean up their act. A clumsy disclaimer proclaiming that Sarandon's character had been tested for AIDS and was engaging in safe sex was fortunately cut early in the editing process. There were also some tense moments as studio honchos insisted that Sarandon's character not be shown drinking a beer in a movie theater while, ironically, they kept in a sequence in which Sarandon and Spader are driving drunk and crash into a mailbox.

Unfortunately, *White Palace* would ultimately fall victim to the prevailing *Pretty Woman* syndrome that was compromising Hollywood at the time. In the wake of that film, every story, no matter how downbeat, had to end with an old-fashioned happy ending, which in the case of *White Palace* was contrary to the novel and the original script's downbeat ending.

The ending of the shooting script had been altered several times and, to make matters worse, the studio was determined to test screen the movie well in advance of the release date. The feedback from these screenings succeeded only in confusing the issue and delaying the release of the film until 1990. Sarandon angrily recalled that she and the rest of the cast were shooting a number of new endings right up until two weeks before the release of the film which would finally open to mixed reviews and unspectacular box office.

"It's frustrating," she reflected. "You put your guts out there on the line; then finally somebody takes your entrails and puts them before the public."

Sarandon's career continued on in a sort of never-never land that seemed to keep stardom just beyond her grasp. She would later say that by the late eighties, the now forty-something actress was in a rut.

Sarandon was invariably the actress who received an early draft of a script that the producers assured her could be rewritten if she was interested or a script in which a male figure played the lead and the woman was there only as a secondary character. That was pretty much the scenario when during this period she was offered the female lead in the movie *Sweet Hearts Dance*.

The film, which starred Don Johnson, then in the mid-stages of trying to forge a movie career after the small-screen success of *Miami Vice*, had the interesting premise of focusing on parallel love stories; one character falling in love while the other tries to keep his failing marriage together. Sarandon liked the premise and the fact that her role of the long-suffering wife exhibited some strength and substance. But what she discovered upon reporting to the film's Vermont location was what she felt was yet another round of Hollywood deception.

A total of forty pages of the script she had agreed to do had been totally rewritten. In place of a rather substantial dramatic story was now a standard-issue buddy film.

Sarandon blew her top. Reports emanating from the set of *Sweet Hearts Dance* related that Sarandon walked off the film at one point and that she engaged in a number of shouting matches with the producer and director. It was also rumored that Sarandon and Johnson had an offscreen affair during the making of that film, something the actress dismissed as preposterous and categorically denied.

For Sarandon, *Sweet Hearts Dance* was mirroring the unpleasantness of *The Witches of Eastwick*. But the difference was that she had learned from that experience. Legally she could do nothing so she went ahead and did her best on what had become yet another dubious addition to her résumé.

By all accounts, Sarandon was emotionally burned out after the completion of *Sweet Hearts Dance*. She was tired of going from picture to picture with high ideals, only to have her sincerity and commitment dashed. She was also frustrated at her seeming inability to capitalize on her successes, a pattern that had repeated itself with regularity over the years.

Sarandon was angry and frustrated at this latest effort gone bad. So much so that, in a rare shift in attitude, she decided to be totally mercenary and do something strictly for the money rather than for any endearing artistic elements. She chose the serial killer-thriller *The January Man*, which had the extra incentive of starring her old friend Kevin Kline. Her role, that of a bitch of a woman who looked like she had seen better physical and emotional days, was largely window dressing and she knew it. Sarandon, however, found the experience less of a chore and more of a fun exercise in which she learned quite a bit from watching her costars Kline, Harvey Keitel, and Rod Steiger work.

"I wasn't operating under the burden of sincerity," she recalled in *Mother Jones*. "I wasn't laboring under the mantle of unfolding the plot. Being totally irresponsible is so liberating."

However, being totally irresponsible was not something that Sarandon could tolerate for long and so, after the completion of *The January Man*, she once again went with her instincts and her politics.

She narrated a television documentary called *AIDS: The Facts of Life* that attempted to explode the myths about AIDS and educate people to the realities of the disease. In a phase where she was wearing her politics on her sleeve, Sarandon journeyed to Zimbabwe to play a South African journalist struggling with her own feelings about apartheid in the wake of the murder of her black gardener's son in the film *A Dry White Season*.

One would have to go all the way back to *Joe* to find a more overtly political film on Sarandon's résumé but, unlike *Joe*, *A Dry White Season* was completely in sync with the actress's political views. She also found it attractive because it gave her the opportunity to be in a film with one of her idols, Marlon Brando. Sarandon was willing to literally work for minimum wage on a project she felt was more than the typical ham-fisted message film.

"I felt it was an important story," she told the *Progressive*. "It's about South Africa but it is also broader. It's about people not wanting to see the truth because it will completely inconvenience their lives."

As befitting a glorified art film, *A Dry White Season* received so-so notices with the emphasis on a spirited performance by Brando. And, for better or worse, critics took notice of Sarandon's limited part. The *New York Times* noticed, "Susan Sarandon has little to do. Her presence suggests a halfhearted attempt at commercialism." *Variety* offered an evenhanded assessment that, "The actress is given no opportunity to do anything but demonstrate a competent Anglo accent."

Personally and professionally, the last half of the eighties was for Sarandon quite simply *Bull Durham*. The film finally succeeded in catapulting Sarandon away from the pack and into the rarefied atmosphere of Hollywood royalty. That it would also cement her personal life was a bonus for the actress who took the first steps in a midlife odyssey of craft and heart. There continued to be stumbles and disappointments but *Bull Durham* and *A Dry White Season* more than balanced Sarandon's cinematic ledger.

Perhaps because of the emotion expended in *A Dry*

141

White Season, Sarandon returned to the States politically energized and got right into the middle of a highly unpopular cause—opposition to the Persian Gulf War.

In fact, with the images of American POWs being dragged through the streets of Baghdad on the nightly news and the evil of Saddam Hussein a constant presence on the world stage, U.S. involvement in the Persian Gulf had become a popular spectator sport, making CNN a media presence.

A grumbling came from the left that President George Bush had started the war to deflect attention from a coming recession. But the world was in a funny place in the late 1980s. Primitive jingoism had replaced rational thought. The Persian Gulf conflict had succeeded in resurrecting a hard-hat mentality in which people wrapped themselves in the American flag. This was not an issue to be on the wrong side of and the perceived right side was far right.

Dissenters from the Hollywood community were in short supply which is why on a sunny January day, the celebrity contingent of an anti–Persian Gulf War crowd estimated at between 75,000 and 300,000 could be counted on two hands with a couple of fingers left over.

Protest veterans Dick Gregory, Bella Abzug, and Peter Yarrow were there. But this being a popular war, Hollywood was barely represented. Actress Margot Kidder, who a couple of weeks earlier took some heat for what was perceived as an anti-POW comment, was standing amid the crowd and placards. So were Sarandon and Robbins.

Sarandon, dressed in black stretch pants, a sweater, dark glasses, and a floppy hat, had done her homework. She had discovered early on parallels between Central America and the Persian Gulf. Through her association with the organization Military Families Support Network, an antiwar group made up of relatives of Persian Gulf soldiers, Sarandon would hear the stories of the Gulf War syndrome and she did not have to look far to see the parallels with Vietnam. She saw the cause of the support network as just. Which was why, hands linked with Robbins and Kidder, she was preparing to march on Washington.

But she was also lighthearted in the face of the protest. She joked to fellow marchers that the whole scene was looking very sixties and laughed that there was the scent of patchouli in the air.

As the crowd marched down Pennsylvania Avenue toward the Capitol steps, the assembled media instinctively gravitated toward Sarandon. Scattered visibly throughout the crowd were law-enforcement officers bent on not letting the demonstration get out of hand, yet knowing full well that they might have to make a celebrity arrest or two.

One photographer snapped Sarandon's picture and then walked up to her and shook her hand.

"You've got a lot of guts," the photographer was quoted in an *American Film* article.

Sarandon smiled.

"Thanks. I hope you'll cover me when I can't work."

c h a p t e r   s i x
"IT WAS A VERY SCARY TIME"

Susan Sarandon need not have feared Hollywood reprisals at that point.

In the Hollywood parlance, Sarandon had somehow sneaked under the radar into the realm of bankable. Her politics, while rarely appreciated by studio executives, were more than balanced by research that indicated a profit-making number of moviegoers would automatically buy a ticket for anything with Susan Sarandon.

The irony was not lost on the actress. It was typical Hollywood. The old adage "You'll never work in this town again . . . until we need you" was never truer. Knowing that, Sarandon could laugh at the power she suddenly wielded.

Susan Sarandon was moving gracefully through middle age. In 1991, at age forty-five Sarandon, who in the coming years would give birth to her second child with Robbins, a boy named Miles, was comfortable, if occasionally frustrated, with her career. Hollywood still treated her with little respect but she could regularly count on salaries

145

reportedly ranging from $500,000 to $1.5 million to keep her comfortable and selective.

With Robbins much more amenable to what was being offered him, and as Sarandon would often report, more willing than she to do blatantly commercial work, Sarandon was free to set the bar high for the film work she did accept. And as Hollywood was discovering these days, the best way to land the actress was with a good part in a good film that would be filmed in New York so that Sarandon would not have to venture far from home and her children.

The reality was that Sarandon was finding peace and compromise in this period. She was committed to her career, perhaps more so than at any other time in her life. But there was also a sense that her job was also at home. In later years, she would often acknowledge that making sure the grocery shopping is done and the toilet paper roll is replaced were very important things in her life. In the most meaningful sense of motherhood versus career, Sarandon could not see herself being away from her family for any length of time.

Which once again put her in personal and professional conflict. She again offered that she had never been incredibly hungry in her approach to her career. Sarandon has offered that it was a fabulous job and that she was lucky to be making a living as an actress but that her career had never been a driving force in her life.

Consequently, Sarandon remained quite content with her personal life. And in particular the obvious commitment from Robbins which, in hindsight, was part and parcel of the fact that she was comfortable and assured in the fact that she was, indeed, getting older. She would often joke that she did not have stretch marks because she was so old when she had her kids that there was nothing left to stretch.

"Nowadays, I think I look lived-in," she said. "When I was younger, I looked blank. Just blank, interchangeable with other people. Now I don't think there's anybody who looks like me."

Given her high-profile stature, Sarandon easily pushed another media hot button, the idea of women having children later in life. Sarandon wholeheartedly recommended the practice and indicated that she had already accomplished much of what she had set out to do professionally and so had no regrets about stopping to have another child. She jokingly told one reporter that while she was vastly "overqualified" for what she did, "you can never be overqualified for parenting."

That Sarandon would willingly bring two children into the world when over the age of forty was groundbreaking stuff at the time. Her decision to expand her family relatively late in life was based largely on the fact that her expectations of family were much different from what her mother's had been.

"What I want for my kids is different from what my mother was trying for. I didn't have my kids when I was young. I had a life first."

During this period, the actress-activist was also

evolving as a political animal. Where she once considered herself apolitical but involved on what she considered a pedestrian level, she was now more than willing to take advantage of her celebrity if the cause was just. She felt she could play the game. There was no risk of career damage by expressing a political opinion. She already knew the media was treating her as a commodity and so she might as well take advantage of the situation to get her points across.

Politically and socially, Sarandon was beginning to cast her net in ever-widening circles. She began actively to monitor the two 1992 presidential candidates and found neither to be particularly kind to her issues. The Republican's choice, the incumbent president George Bush Sr., she saw as an out-and-out "fascist" who had to be defeated at all costs.

But in the Democratic nominee, Bill Clinton, she saw a different kind of enemy. She deemed Clinton "gutless" on what she considered the major issue: our escalating presence in the Persian Gulf that, to many deep thinkers, had Vietnam written all over it. As always, Sarandon had done her homework and had come to the conclusion that Clinton, all smiles and camera-friendly hair and face, was shallow where it counted.

"I think that Clinton is probably a vote to save the Supreme Court," she told the *Los Angeles Times* in 1992. "But I'm furious with the Democratic Party because at a time when the country has such clear-cut problems and when issues could have been really dealt with in a different way than the Republicans have, we've got the closest thing to a Republican in Clinton."

Such an observation was not uncommon on Sarandon's part. If nothing else, the years had hardened her to going with her instincts when it came to her political views. And so, while her views were easily more in line with the more liberal wing of the Democratic Party, she was, at heart, a classic independent who was more than willing to cross lines if the cause was right.

True to her principles, when the Democrats invited Sarandon to speak at the Democratic convention, she politely but forcefully declined the invitation. Many perceived the slight as a tactical error on Sarandon's part. With the eyes of the world literally and figuratively on the convention, this seemed the perfect opportunity for Sarandon to air her agenda, particularly as it related to our questionable policies abroad. But Sarandon was insistent that she did not want to muddy her own platform by even giving the hint of being behind a party that she knew was soft on the things she cared about.

Over the years, Hollywood had alternately tolerated and was amused by Sarandon's activism. But her and Robbins's increased vocal activity on behalf of the anti–Persian Gulf War factions was running contrary to Hollywood's new testosterone-driven pro-war stance. The couple had often heard the whispers that their careers might have been further along if they had politically leaned a bit more to the right. They had never paid those stories much mind. But when Sarandon and Robbins

joined other speakers in Washington, D.C., in 1991 to educate the politicians on the fact that not everybody was in
favor of the Gulf War, Sarandon sensed she was crossing a
mighty big line.

"The message was clear," she recalled in a *Buzz* interview. "Any kind of dissent is going to be problematic. It was
alarming to me that so many people who you could count
on before had bought this thing about 'you can't support
the troops if you ask questions.' That was very scary.
People were frightened for us. I was frightened for us."

And with good reason. Much like Vietnam, people were
quick to choose up sides when it came to the Persian Gulf
conflict and, as Sarandon would discover, celebrity was not
a shield. One day Sarandon was accosted on the street by
what she described as a "huge stranger businessman"
while protesting the war. She remembered being called
everything in the book. And she remembered being scared.

"It was a scary time. It was the only time I felt so alone,
taking a stand on something and looked around and
nobody else was there."

Sarandon continued to entertain film offers and, not
surprisingly, most of what she was getting was not of overriding interest. Because, for better or worse, Sarandon had
become a type, a world-weary cynical type in particular,
which was fine with her if the scripts had substance.
Unfortunately much of these offerings would have her
thrashing around in a weak storyline and playing an
obvious caricature of what she had done before.

Sarandon was becoming increasingly concerned that

her catalogue of eccentric portrayals was having the opposite effect on her career and that people without passion or insight were automatically assuming she could just play herself in just about anything and make it work.

And then there was *Thelma & Louise*.

There had been films with feminist themes before but nothing that compared to this emotionally and psychologically apocalyptic tale of two lifelong friends, a dissatisfied housewife fleeing a dominating husband, and a middle-aged waitress in a dead-end relationship, who decide to hit the road for a vacation from their lives, only to discover violence and a side of themselves they never knew existed.

On paper this was a provocative, distaff look at a climate of fear and persecution and what happens when two basically decent, law-abiding women get caught up in it, turn it inside out, and become both a victim of it—and the cure. Freud would have a field day with *Thelma & Louise*. Hollywood hoped to as well.

On the surface *Thelma & Louise* was, in the Hollywood vernacular, a feminist buddy movie, essentially a Bonnie and Clyde take updated to the nineties as Bonnie and Bonnie. But Sarandon, with her political and social radar always on the alert, saw the important messages laying within the subtext of the film.

Sarandon's feelings about *Thelma & Louise* were couched in feminism. She saw the film as a polemic for women to stop settling. In her mind, women had been manipulating men for years to get what they wanted. She felt *Thelma & Louise* would kick open the doors to

151

equality between the sexes and, admittedly, that prospect was pretty scary to the actress.

Sarandon was excited at the rare opportunity for the woman to be a real-world outlaw, literally and figuratively blasting away at preconceived societal demons. That the film was also upfront in its feminism was like icing on the cake. The actress's ego was also tweaked by the fact that the film's director, Ridley Scott, who had shown his mettle at the head of *Alien* and *Blade Runner*, actually wanted her for the role of gun-wielding Louise.

"She's always inventive, continually surprising, and very funny," explained Scott of his preference for Sarandon in the book *Ridley Scott: Close Up*. Scott, who would later make *Gladiator* and *Hannibal*, said, "In fact, Susan's one of the best actresses we've got."

There was only one obstacle to Sarandon saying yes. Not surprisingly, *Thelma & Louise* was causing more than one timid studio executive problems; not the least of which was the fact that the two women die at the end. Sarandon got wind of a possible script change and an upbeat ending and immediately, with visions of *White Palace* still fresh in her head, went to the director.

"The first thing I demanded from the director [Ridley Scott] was that I die in the last scene," she told the *London Independent*. "I didn't want the movie to end with me in Club Med. Once he assured me I was definitely on the death list, I accepted the part."

Thelma & Louise was a physically demanding shoot but one that Sarandon instinctively gravitated toward. "It's kind of like joining a cult," she told *Premiere*. "We meet Ridley in a desolate area, get in a car, drive eight hours in the blistering sun, and finally just surrender to his judgment."

Sarandon had admittedly expected the worst on *Thelma & Louise*. Logistically, shooting in the American Southwest could be nothing but a nightmare. But while the filming, replete with car chases, gunplay, and explosions, was arduous, it was easily one of the most controlled, smooth-running sets Sarandon had ever been on.

"For a while, we never even got dirty," she recalled. "I had to call a meeting. 'Ridley,' I said, 'we've got to get dirty.'"

While never what would be termed a method actress, Sarandon found that she could slip into the role of road rebel Louise with relative ease. Scott's initial enthusiasm for the actress continued as he allowed Sarandon an inordinate amount of freedom to mold the character into her own vision. And, in other situations, Sarandon candidly admitted, "Ridley and I fought about things. We changed scenes."

Specifically she added lines in the scene with the verbally abusive truck driver and, with the aid of Tim Robbins who, with the children, was visiting on the set, she rewrote her love scene when she found it too cliché and frilly.

Despite the presence of such veteran actors as Harvey Keitel and Michael Madsen, Sarandon was the one who the relative newcomers Geena Davis and Brad Pitt turned to for advice, and the actress, often jokingly, reveled in the role of set matriarch. A sure sign, she often said, that she was truly getting old.

Costar Geena Davis recalled in an *Inside the Actors*

Studio interview how Sarandon used her power on the set to bail her out of an uncomfortable situation during the making of the film. As mentioned earlier, director Ridley Scott requested that Davis take her shirt off during the filming of one scene.

"I thought this was a bad idea but I didn't say so. We broke for lunch and I ran over to Susan and said, 'What am I going to do? Ridley wants me to take my shirt off in this scene.' She said, 'Oh for heaven's sake, Ridley, Geena is not going to take her shirt off in this scene.' He said, 'Okay, okay.' "

Sarandon was particularly enamored of the moments in the film when Louise, in a visceral rage, used guns and other forms of violence to lash out at the primarily male-driven evils in the world. She recalled in a *Los Angeles Times* interview that the scene in which she blows away the man who had attempted to rape Thelma was a particularly important one in terms of tying all the emotional and psychological threads of the film together.

"The thing that worked for me was more her [Sarandon's character] being in jeopardy than conjuring up some old outrage. I felt like it was more that she just wanted to shut him up. But then when he says whatever he says, that pushes her over the top and she goes to shut him up. But the impulse was just to erase that insult rather than to assassinate him."

And with her penchant for finding challenges at every turn, Sarandon emerged from *Thelma & Louise* with a new element of her acting persona.

"In that movie, mainly what I had to do was drive and

listen," she told the *Washington Post*. "I had to concentrate on keeping the car in a certain relationship to the camera truck. Geena had all the lines. I was just concentrating on driving and occasionally replying. And somehow that would work. And I realized from that, you can do your best work when you're concentrating on something else."

The inherent controversy surrounding *Thelma & Louise* carried over to Sarandon in the wake of the film's completion. Even before the film was released in 1991, Sarandon was being talked up as a sure Best Actress nominee at Oscar time.

The all-important perception in Hollywood at that time was that the actress, at age forty-five, had finally arrived as a full-fledged superstar.

Critics jumped into the center of the perceived controversy surrounding *Thelma & Louise* but also managed to find space to laud Sarandon for a first-rate performance. The *Nation* stated, "Sarandon lets you sense what's going on behind the waspishness." The *Los Angeles Times* credited, "Both actresses run through a gamut of emotions that is formidable in its richness." The *Hollywood Reporter* added, "Sarandon plays what could have been a stereotypical character and invests her with depth and sensual appeal." Sarandon's depth of character was noticed by the *Long Beach Press Telegram*, "Sarandon is the earthy anchor who expects and finds the worst in everyone."

Sarandon took the accolades graciously and retreated back into a relatively quiet home life with her three children and Tim.

By contrast to her glamorous occupation, Sarandon and Robbins's home life had been so normal that the couple remained fairly unaffected by the fishbowl nature of celebrity. They would regularly venture out in public alone or as a family unit and their demeanor had been so normal that they were inevitably treated with respect. Eminently approachable, the couple would (and still) oblige autograph requests under most circumstances . . . except when it impacted on their family.

Robbins related that they were once out with their family when they were approached by somebody requesting an autograph. Sarandon and Robbins said it was all right with them if it was all right with their children. In this case, their children did have a problem with it and so Sarandon and Robbins politely refused and explained why. The autograph seeker went away empty-handed but, in the face of the couple's low-key and democratic approach to their family, seemed far from disappointed.

But despite these occasional intrusions in their private life, Sarandon and Robbins insisted on not putting on the expected Hollywood airs. In an interview, Sarandon explained that there was a definite reason for keeping their lives normal.

Sarandon had always felt herself a part of the real world and that once she began walking the streets with bodyguards and an entourage people would notice her. And she did not want to project an image that she was afraid of people.

That Robbins had gravitated so naturally toward

fatherhood was a joy for Sarandon to observe. He was the perfect surrogate father for Eva who was well into her teens. Robbins and the boys would spend hours out on the sidewalk in front of their home playing baseball or whatever sport happened to be in season.

"I'm the one who says, 'It's time to come in now, it's getting late,' " she laughingly explained to the *Herald Sun*. "And he can just play for hours. Sometimes he has to remind me to just forget about it and join in the game. But someone has to nag them and say 'no.' But maybe it's a good match because of that."

Sarandon, along with Robbins, was a constant presence for a number of causes in the early nineties. She continued to be in the forefront of the AIDS fight and, with rare exceptions such as Elizabeth Taylor, was the only big-time Hollywood celebrity willing to step forward. Sarandon was candid in saying that a scarcity of Hollywood, and in particular top-name male muscle, was the by-product of fear and prejudice that lurks below Hollywood's alleged philanthropic image.

"Recently somebody called me for an AIDS benefit and said, 'We need a guy. We need someone from the real Hollywood community,' " she said in a candid *Playboy* interview. "A lot of male actors are afraid that if they support AIDS fund-raising, they'll be known as gay and then they won't work. The horrible thing is that it's a legitimate fear."

Her involvement in AIDS issues soon led Sarandon to discover the near-epidemic proportions the disease had visited on the people of other countries. Haiti, in particular, has been devastated by the disease and the epidemic was being compounded by the fact that many HIV-infected refugees, attempting to flee the country and its oppressive government, were being incarcerated by the U.S. government at its Guantánamo Bay Naval Base in Cuba. Amnesty International called the conditions inhuman. Hunger strikes were rampant among the imprisoned and ill Haitians, and many were dying because of their protests. Once again Sarandon saw injustice and let her voice be heard.

She participated in many of the earliest U.S. demonstrations against the Haitian detainment and, during one such protest in New York, was arrested. The protests succeeded in calling attention to the problems at Guantánamo and the fact that it was U.S. tax dollars that were supporting what she perceived as a barbaric practice.

But the U.S. government insisted that nothing illegal or life threatening was going on. The media went along with this explanation and did not protest when requests to go on the naval base were denied. Sarandon fumed at the lack of journalistic guts on the part of the media regarding the Haitians and their continued kid-glove treatment of the military when it came to the escalating of the Persian Gulf War.

Consequently she was primed to take on the journalism profession when she began a round of press interviews shortly before the Memorial Day release of *Thelma & Louise*. She was particularly vitriolic during an interview with the *Washington Post* when she verbally chastised the reporter for not being more aggressive in pursuing the Persian Gulf War story.

"The Persian Gulf War will stand as a low point in American journalism," she said. "To accept without any outrage these limitations just from the point of historical gathering of information is alarming. I just don't understand what you people could have thought. Nobody checked a thing. You just bought into the myth that the war was inevitable and that it was saving people."

Earlier in her career, those kinds of remarks would have been dutifully noted but most likely would not see print. But Sarandon's celebrity now put her in the exploitable range by the press, even if it meant printing barbs against their own profession. Sarandon savored the power to manipulate and publicize that had come to her and was quick to take advantage of it whenever she could.

Thelma & Louise opened to rave reviews, good box office, and the expected controversy. Many male viewers were repulsed at the notion of a couple of women invading their testosterone-laden action turf. Sarandon was amused at the reaction but agreed, in a *Los Angeles Times* interview, that this response was inevitable and quite understandable.

"I don't think we understand how firmly the heterosexual white male was holding onto that territory of heroic movie maleness. To make women a little out of control and have violence as an option, to give a woman a gun and to have her feel things that excessively. Nobody wants to see that."

But women and, yes, men did see Sarandon's gun-toting, no-nonsense, modern-day gunslinger as an apocalyptic image of the changing times. The accolades were

159

coming thick and fast, as was the certainty of another Best Actress nomination for Sarandon. But after losing the Oscar for *Atlantic City* and *Bull Durham* (and crying for days afterward), Sarandon, who found much disdain in what she perceived as a shallow, self-congratulatory exercise, was not thrilled at the announcement.

She sarcastically offered the insight that the awards process gets easier the more you don't win. And sure enough, come Oscar night, Sarandon once again walked away empty-handed. But Sarandon and Geena Davis were both so good that they likely split the vote.

Sarandon's post–*Thelma & Louise* choices flew in the face of the growing perception of her as a superstar. Rather than jump into another high-profile Hollywood epic, Sarandon turned, instead, to a series of small roles and quirky leads. In the political satire *Bob Roberts*, which starred Tim Robbins in this tale of the coming-of-age of a right-wing political candidate, Sarandon played the role of acerbic television news anchor Tawna Titan in the outrageous send-up of Hollywood.

But easily the strangest choice was the role of a yuppie drug dealer in the film *Light Sleeper*. Sarandon has often described herself as being old school and organic when it comes to drug use; strictly a pot and mushrooms person in days gone by, and antidrugs in general now, she saw nothing political in the choice. Her reasoning for doing *Light Sleeper* was to destroy the stereotype being perpetuated in films that drugs are always connected with people of color.

"It's quite liberating to play someone who's slightly nasty and not burdened with sincerity," she related in *Time Out*. "It's fun to have a woman as the boss and everybody else is working for her."

Ironically, the small film would end up giving Sarandon some of her best notices. The *Los Angeles Times* said, "Sarandon walks off with this picture. Her character is comic, lusty, and magnificently at home." *Variety* peppered its review with superlatives, "The actress is lively and quick-witted as usual." *Elle* described, "Her glamorously tough, self-aware Anne gives the movie a transfusion of vitality anytime she appears."

With its decided parallel to the AIDS epidemic, it came as no surprise that Sarandon was interested in *Lorenzo's Oil*, the tale of an educated couple's search for the cure for their son's disease. It was also the opportunity to work with an actor she admired, Nick Nolte. But there were obstacles. The consensus in Hollywood was that Michelle Pfeiffer, who seemed up for everything these days, was about to say yes to the role. Adding intrigue to the mix was the fact that the film's director was George Miller, the director whom she held responsible for making her life a living hell on *The Witches of Eastwick* and against whom she still held a grudge.

"But I liked the script and the story," she acknowledged in the *New York Daily News*. "So whether or not I get along with someone personally or respect them as a person, isn't as important as if they have a vision. And Miller had a vision and felt passionately about telling that story."

161

When Pfeiffer unexpectedly dropped out of the project, Miller turned to Sarandon and, according to the actress, "begged me to do it." Sarandon accepted. But not without some trepidation. She refused to get into a conversation that would clear the air about the horror that was *The Witches of Eastwick*. She felt that would be too painful and ultimately not productive.

"I just felt what had happened, had happened and it just made me very cautious of him, it made it very hard for me to trust him," she told *Film Comment*. "But I felt I knew who George was and what his weaknesses and strengths were. So I asked him just to explain to me why he wanted to do this and how he saw it. So I was forewarned about when I could count on him and when I couldn't."

This was obviously a project fraught with problems and given her attitude toward director Miller, one has to wonder why she would enter into a creative pact with somebody she so totally distrusted. This was Sarandon taking a big risk, one in which she hoped the creative rewards would outweigh her basic dislike of the director. Consequently, everybody was on high alert during the first days of filming, looking for what they felt would be the inevitable clash between Sarandon and Miller—a clash that surprisingly never came to pass.

What made the working arrangement so good was that she discovered that Miller felt that the key to *Lorenzo's Oil* was the search for the medicine. Which meant Sarandon would be pretty much on her own in developing and projecting her character. This was not necessarily the best time for Sarandon to be left to her own devices in a story in which a child's life was at stake. She was pregnant at the time and, during the filming, she would experience horrible nightmares in which the reality of her own being and that of her fictional counterpart were emotionally and psychologically entangled.

Under the circumstances, Sarandon chose a subtle approach to acting in the film, which entailed being naturally open to the realism of the story. Having an actor of Nick Nolte's stature playing opposite her was a key to the project's success.

Lorenzo's Oil turned out to be a solid portrayal for the now forty-five-year-old Sarandon. Her role of a mother on a mission was devoid of the clichés inherent in the weepy story line and full of the quiet, straightforward passion that had become a Sarandon trademark. It was a total about-face from *Thelma & Louise* but, following on the heels of the quirky *Light Sleeper* and *Bob Roberts*, it cemented Sarandon's reputation as an actress capable of straddling all nuances of the acting spectrum. Yet another Oscar nomination followed but Sarandon was not surprised when, in 1992, she once again missed out on the top prize.

While not surprised, the snubbing at Oscar time for a series of award-winning performances was beginning to get old. Sarandon had an ego and the continued slights were a constant irritation. In her private moments, the actress had to be wondering what she had to do to finally get the Academy nod.

163

SUSAN SARANDON

Sarandon returned to her family and politics. Of the latter, she was in a particularly active period in her life, going to bat for a number of causes including First Amendment rights and her ongoing involvement with AIDS. She continued to maintain that her home life with Robbins and their blended family was fairly traditional in that they and their children spent a lot of time doing what most traditional family units do. But politics, especially as they pertain to their daily lives, was also an intregal part of their daily routine.

In Robbins's and her world, taxes were paid, children were cared for, the environment was discussed, and friends were dying of AIDS. Sarandon reasoned that in a world where homelessness was literally outside their door, a passion for politics was primarily a form of self-defense.

On the personal front, Sarandon and Robbins continued to form the perfect bond. Spiritually and emotionally they seemed ideally suited for each other.

Going on seven years together, they seemed, like another celebrated couple, Kurt Russell and Goldie Hawn, to have defied the odds in their unorthodox relationship. Sarandon would often jokingly concede that it was not always smooth sailing, however.

"It's not exactly what I'd call a calm relationship all the time. But we don't spend a lot of time worrying whether there's somebody out there who would be better."

Given the collective mind-set of Robbins and Sarandon, it was not a leap that their children would become equally aware of the importance of being involved

164

in the world. From the beginning, Sarandon made it plain that she and Tim wanted their children to see their parents as people who were passionately committed to causes. That it took became very evident one day when the family was discussing politics. Daughter Eva was particularly taken with Robbins's political fervor. She smiled, recalled Sarandon, and said, "I guess this means another march in Washington, hey Mom?"

Despite an erratic professional career, Sarandon had succeeded in cultivating a loyal following, one built on her obvious acting talents as well as on her ability to consistently gravitate toward risky and often unorthodox roles. This modus operandi was very much the case for Sarandon in the first half of the nineties as she, possibly for the first time, found her choices guided largely by political and social themes. There was an obvious growth in terms of the films Sarandon chose to do in the nineties. She was not settling for cinematic fluff anymore but rather was insisting on films that had substance. She had arrived as an accomplished actress.

But with the exception of her Oscar nominations, Sarandon was rarely recognized for her work and so the actress was unabashedly thrilled when she was honored with a film retrospective and the Piper Heidsieck achievement award at the prestigious Boston Film Festival.

Days later she joked about the idea of receiving the honors at the ripe old age of forty-five. "I feel so old! But better they do it now than when I'm not lucid!"

A big topic of conversation at the Sarandon-Robbins dinner table remained the plight of the imprisoned Haitians in Guantánamo Bay. After a rush of publicity, it became old news and was quickly slipping from the public's consciousness. Sarandon reasoned that it would take something on a massive scale to put the topic back in the mind of middle America. The 1993 Academy Award ceremonies seemed like the perfect platform to reignite passions.

Although neither Sarandon nor Robbins were up for an award, their status as a power couple had paved their way to the upper level of guest presenters and they had agreed to face the television cameras and millions of viewers to present the Best Film Editing Award. They logically reasoned that any kind of dissent at the Academy Awards would be problematic, given the current political climate in Hollywood, and there was the always hovering specter of negative repercussions for their careers. But in the end, they felt compelled to speak out against a grave injustice whatever the fallout.

Oscar show producer Gil Cates sensed that there might be some problems as he set about planning the evening's Oscar telecast. With the feature-length documentary *The Panama Deception* considered by many a sure thing for Best Documentary and the likes of such politically charged activists as Sarandon, Robbins, and Richard Gere as presenters, he felt the Academy Awards could easily dissolve into an uncomfortable series of political statements. And so he took precautions.

Cates met with all the presenters individually and went over the show's script with them to make sure they had no problems with what they were supposed to say.

Cates was relieved until the day of the Oscars when he got wind of the fact that Sarandon and Robbins were going to drop a political bombshell on Oscar night. He immediately called up the couple's public relations representative and angrily warned that Sarandon and Robbins better not make any political statements.

The audience for the Academy Awards ceremony was awash in red ribbons, an encouraging sign that AIDS had finally struck a chord with the Hollywood community. And, as they waited their turn as presenters, Sarandon was well aware that behind many of those same ribbons were people who were HIV positive or knew somebody who was. Sarandon was nervous, but she was sure Robbins and she were about to do the right thing.

"I've never been so terrified to disrupt things," she told *Buzz*. "But I felt it was completely appropriate. It was not an issue of whether or not these Haitians could come into the country. It was about whether HIV was going to be called a crime."

Word had gotten around regarding Sarandon and Robbins's plans and so there was a mixture of polite applause and silent apprehension when the couple strode before the cameras to announce the Best Editing nominations and winner. They glanced down at the teleprompter—and spoke their mind.

Robbins began by saying, "In the spirit of the red ribbons being held here, we'd like to call attention to 250 Haitians being held in Cuba. Their crime, testing positive for the HIV virus."

167

SUSAN SARANDON

A scattering of boos and angry shouts rained down on the couple as Sarandon asked U.S. government officials to admit the refugees to the United States. Twenty-six seconds after they began their speech, it was over.

"Hearing people shouting at us was terrifying," recalled Sarandon in a *New York Daily News* article. "I could barely breathe. I was so scared. But I don't think I could have lived with myself if I hadn't done it."

Silence and angry looks greeted the couple as they made their way through the wings and back to their seats. Many people averted their eyes, refusing to look at the couple. A brave few openly embraced the couple for their courage. But the majority simply turned their backs. The repercussions were not long in coming. The very next day, the papers were full of angry denouncements by Hollywood bigwigs.

Bob Rehme, president of the Academy of Motion Picture Arts and Sciences, angrily said that the show is about movies. "It's not supposed to be about political activities around the world no matter how much individually we might support any one of those causes."

Producer Gil Cates also denounced Sarandon and Robbins's actions. "For someone who I invite to present an award to use that time to postulate a personal political belief I think is not only outrageous, it's distasteful and dishonest."

In response to these attacks and others, Sarandon and Robbins wrote an impassioned letter that appeared in the entertainment section of the *Los Angeles Times* in which

168

they defended their actions, explained the realities of the Guantánamo Bay Haitian situation, and ended the letter with the question, "Was what we did inappropriate? We think that silence in the face of cruelty is truly inappropriate."

But while there would be scattered pockets of support for their actions, the response from Hollywood was decidedly negative. Cates stated that they would never appear in any capacity on an Oscar show again. Sarandon acknowledged that Robbins and she had received a lot of hate mail and threatening phone calls in the wake of their Oscar-night speech. And not too far from the surface was the very real threat of being blackballed by the industry.

Robbins remained stubbornly neutral in the face of the growing praise for Sarandon's and his actions, insisting that he did not want people to be either "inspired or offended" by what they did.

But, at the end of the day, Sarandon felt their actions were worth any possible damage to their careers.

"I had been a presenter for years and years and I hadn't talked about things," she explained to the *Hollywood Reporter*. "But I felt this was an emergency. I just felt that there was no other choice. The right to speak out is what's great about this country."

ACLU executive director Ira Glasser heard about Susan and Tim's courageous public stand and applauded them for it.

"Basically what Susan and Tim did is they got a huge audience. They were prepared to present themselves as something more than the glitter. It always depends on how

169

well you pull it off. Tim and Susan are serious people who are willing to use their assets for serious things that they believe in. There are so few people who are willing to stand up for unpopular civil liberty issues that you've got to applaud them."

Susan Sarandon had made her point. The day after the Oscar speech, it was announced that the United States government was releasing the Haitian refugees.

c h a p t e r s e v e n
"I ALREADY KNOW WHAT I THINK"

While she had, figuratively speaking, won the war, Sarandon had suffered her share of battlefield wounds.

A lot of so-called friends were suddenly not returning her calls. The rumors were flying thick and fast that major Hollywood studio heads were banding together to deny Sarandon and Robbins work. And a lot of people she did not even know had discovered her address and were sending her hate mail.

"Some of them were particularly vile and thoughtless. One said, 'Why didn't I have some of those sick faggots into my own home with my illegitimate children?' "

Notorious for having a tough hide when it came to her political and social stands, Sarandon would often acknowledge, in the wake of their Academy Awards speech, that she was emotionally taken aback by the viciousness of these personal attacks. She could understand honest disagreement and sensed that the anger was the by-product of mere ignorance and extreme shortsidedness. But, she reasoned, that was seemingly yet another by-product of the growing political and social schism in America. However, she was not dissuaded and would continue to speak out in support of AIDS and Central American issues whenever possible.

For the next year Sarandon would be denounced by the conservative press and radio talk-show hosts as being an overaged hippie who was out of touch with the prevailing attitudes of the country. However, while the rumors continued to abound that Sarandon was now being blackballed by the industry for her political stance, the reality was that, although continuing to receive scripts, she was finding nothing to entice her to leave a period of domestic bliss in which the simple act of shuttling her two children (and toddler, Miles, who was born in 1991) back and forth to school was more satisfying than the possibilities of the roles she was being offered.

Sarandon was effusive in her praise for domesticity in an *Entertainment Weekly* interview. "If I were twenty-two and trying to build a career, I don't know who'd be watching the kids as happily as I do. It takes so much to get me to break out of domestic paradise. There's hardly anything that interests me as much as my family."

This was just as well because even in this advanced stage of her career, Sarandon was still finding herself being treated shabbily by the industry. While not going into specifics on the current round of slights, Sarandon has acknowledged on more than one occasion that, even in the wake of her breakout role in *Thelma & Louise*, she was still being offered parts that had already been offered to somebody else and was still being treated like a second-tier actress. It was often speculated that this was the movie industry's way of punishing her for the Oscar-night speech while not driving her completely out of the business.

"They always find a way to humiliate me," she explained in *Entertainment Weekly*. "No matter how successful you are, as an actor you're always vulnerable."

Sarandon's remark was couched in resignation rather than anger. After all these years, there really was no anger left. This was the petty way in which Hollywood always operated and nothing she said or did was going to change it. And so she chose to ignore it.

Susan Sarandon was, by age forty-five, thoroughly happy and quite adept at being fortyish and motherly. In fact, the actress could often be found cracking jokes at her own expense when it came to her new stage in life. The studios were quick to pick up on the notion that not every Susan Sarandon project had to have a political or social hook and that the actress was fully capable of playing old-fashioned and traditional mothers, albeit with an obvious bit of tenacity and edge. Enter the period of mother roles.

Sarandon's agent was uncomfortable with the fact that her client may have finally overcome the vacuous sex symbol role, only to have it replaced with the dreaded motherhood monster. But Sarandon, somewhat surprisingly, ignored her agent's advice and began actively considering those roles. To her way of thinking, playing an older woman or a grandmother was just as creative a challenge as playing a baseball groupie or a gun-toting waitress. She was quite comfortable at the prospect of entering Hollywood's next line of more mature roles.

Sarandon saw such challenges in the remake of the Louisa May Alcott classic *Little Women* in which she would be updating the role of Marmee March, the mother who directed the lives of the title characters during the Civil War. Always looking for the subtext in every role, Sarandon instinctively felt that she understood the ethical and religious perspective of the Alcott story. While remaining true to the book, Sarandon saw the film as an opportunity to make small statements about the lives of young women in the nineties. And with her growing clout in the industry, she felt certain that any suggestions she made on that account would at least be considered.

Indeed, Sarandon's progressive freethinking attitude was brought into play during the filming of *Little Women* in a sequence in which Marmee is warning her daughter that it was not a good idea to show a lot of cleavage or to be flirtatious at a dance. In the original script, the tone was more in keeping with the period, with an emphasis on what other people would think. This to Sarandon rang false. Her research indicated that the Alcotts had never been overly concerned with what other people felt. And so she suggested that the line be changed to reflect the importance of not relying on the superficial to get through life.

In her next film, *Safe Passage*, Sarandon was given the opportunity to play Mag Singer, the mother of seven sons, who was emotionally and spiritually losing control of her life. With its wide range of emotional swings and its world-weary tone, the role seemed tailor-made for the now mature actress. And, although neither *Little Women* nor *Safe Passage* was close to being what most would consider box-office successes, the very act of Sarandon moving in a different direction only served to reinforce the notion that the actress was at the peak of her talents and was literally quite capable of doing anything.

Beyond the acting challenges the two films represented, film historians tend to look upon *Little Women* and *Safe Passage* as an important transitional phase in Sarandon's career. The characters she was playing were patently older and, on the surface, seemed too embellished with historical and style clichés for anyone to add a new believable dimension. Sarandon's portrayals, stark and resonating with a believable level of angst, provided ample evidence that the actress, in later years, was capable of avoiding rote performances and would finally succeed in adding substance to even the most predictable characters.

An acknowledgment of the degree she was revered in the acting community came in 1994 when Sarandon was invited to be on the prestigious television interview program *Inside the Actors Studio*. The show, filmed in the famed New York Actors Studio school in front of an audience of film and acting students, saw Sarandon in her element. Alternately sarcastic and insightful, as well as highly entertaining, Sarandon held the audience in the palm of her hand with tales of her career, specific film anecdotes, and a nod to her political and social activism.

For somebody who was reportedly being blackballed

by the industry (and a fact that was always publicly denied by the studios), Sarandon was quite busy. After completing *Little Women* and *Safe Passage* virtually back-to-back, Sarandon was offered the plumb role of the flawed attorney Reggie Love in the movie adaptation of the John Grisham novel *The Client*.

Although she liked the idea of playing an attorney, Sarandon initially had not expressed much interest in the role. But she realized, with an attitude that indicated she did indeed know film business, that Grisham novels had a history of box-office gold and that to be associated with *The Client* could only enhance her profile, even at this late date, in mainstream Hollywood.

In a slight but dramatic twist on the *Thelma & Louise* scenario, *The Client* director Joel Schumacher courted Sarandon in an overtly theatrical way when, in the middle of a power lunch in a trendy New York restaurant, he got down on one knee and begged Sarandon to do the film. Sarandon was impressed with Schumacher's efforts and overt praise.

Schumacher felt Sarandon was heaven-sent. Reggie Love was no cardboard cutout. The actress who portrayed her had to believably project intelligence, strength, compassion, and vulnerability. And he felt that Sarandon projected all those qualities.

But the reason she decided to do *The Client* turned out to be more personal than professional. It would allow her to work out of town during the summer months which would not disrupt her children's school year. In fact, the convenience of her family had come to be an overriding factor in juggling her personal and professional life. In later years, it had become an unwritten rule that Sarandon would leave the confines of New York for a truly exceptional project and that anybody wanting Sarandon in their film would have a leg up on the competition if its location were in the Big Apple. It was a rule from which Sarandon rarely wavered.

"My kids are so much more interesting than most of the scripts that I read that it's certainly not even tempting to spend more time chasing more work. I'm not tempted that often. So real life to me is much more compelling."

That the script for *The Client* fit her criterion of good story and good character was only part of the positive experience she had on the film (although at her insistence the script was altered slightly so that her character did not seem quite so passive). The other was that Schumacher was so trusting of Sarandon's instincts that he gave her creative license to the extent that Sarandon, at one point, became concerned that the freedom she was being afforded could be problematic and result in an unfocused performance.

In the best possible way, *The Client*'s Reggie Love was typecasting for Sarandon: a character who was, at once, smart and strong and also with a touch of vulnerability lying just below the surface. Historically Sarandon has been at her best when she's had a lot to work with and so it came as no surprise that her portrayal of Reggie Love was being touted as some of her best work to date. It was a performance that went deep into the inner life of her character and thus made the story and the relationships that ultimately unfold a more nuanced and believable experience.

And, as usual, Sarandon was very much a contributing factor to her own success. It had become a given that Sarandon would have an opinion and so it inevitably boiled down to how much a director was willing to bend to accommodate an opinionated star. In the case of director Schumacher, Sarandon was shocked at the ease in which she was able to get his attention.

Schumacher proved the perfect creative for Sarandon. When the actress had a suggestion, the director listened and, more often than not, would incorporate her ideas into the script. In fact, Schumacher was being so receptive to the actress that Sarandon was openly concerned that her portrayal might suffer from self-indulgence.

While on location with *The Client* in New Orleans, Sarandon read some rave reviews about a recently published book entitled *Dead Man Walking*, the true-life story of Sister Helen Prejean, a nun opposed to the death penalty who ministers to a death-row inmate while also embracing the plight of the grieving family of the person he murdered. Sarandon quickly read the book and was struck by the quiet power and integrity of the narrative as well as the questions it posed to her own anti-capital punishment feelings. Sarandon, who had quietly evolved into what would be known as a lapsed Catholic over the years, was moved by the sincerity and persistence in Sister Helen's odyssey and felt she had to meet this woman.

"One afternoon, I'm in the kitchen and the phone rings

and the voice on the other end says, 'Hi. This is Susan Sarandon. I'm in New Orleans. I'm filming *The Client*,'" recalled Sister Helen Prejean in a speech at the Charlottesville Performing Arts Center. " 'I'm reading your book. I'd love to meet you.' I had heard about her from Amnesty International that she was a great human rights advocate so I said great."

For her part, Sister Helen was a bit nervous about dealing with Hollywood. There had been a scattering of interest in making a film of *Dead Man Walking* and she had been cautioned by more than one person that, once she signed a contract, they could turn her serious story into a musical comedy and there would be nothing she could do about it. And so, to get an idea of the person she would be meeting, she rented *Thelma & Louise* and mistakenly reasoned that Geena Davis was Sarandon, which made her even more leery about meeting the actress.

"I kept saying to myself, 'I like Louise. I like Louise.' So when she comes into the restaurant (for our meeting), it was a prayer of Thanksgiving to God out of relief that she was Louise."

Over dinner, Sarandon talked about Tim and her good works, their now infamous Academy Awards speech, and basically painted the quite accurate picture of herself as sincere.

Sarandon's initial concerns about meeting Sister Helen, a nun after all, were immediately laid to rest. She was bright, inquisitive, and wise to the ways of the real world, in other words she was unlike any other nun Sarandon had ever come across. The actress responded with praise for the book and suggested that it would make a wonderful movie.

179

Sarandon completed *The Client* and immediately returned to New York where Robbins, who had recently completed a script for a 1930s censorship fable called *The Cradle Will Rock* which he intended to direct, was attempting, so far unsuccessfully, to get funding for the film. Sarandon insisted that he had to drop everything and option *Dead Man Walking*.

"I wanted to, had to, do the film. I was interested in the death penalty but I wasn't obsessed with it. I was against it because it just didn't make sense."

Robbins read the book and agreed that, indeed, *Dead Man Walking* would make a powerful and, politically and socially, important film—one that he would direct and that Sarandon would star in.

"Susan was the only actress for the role," Robbins told the *Calgary Sun*. "She understands how to go to the heart of a character without resorting to flashy acting."

Sister Helen came to New York and met with Sarandon and Robbins. By this time, the nun had agreed in principle to sign over the rights to *Dead Man Walking* to Susan and Tim. Although admittedly naive to the ways of Hollywood she felt that, in Sarandon, she had found a person of sincerity and trust.

There were immediate, legitimate concerns between Sarandon and Robbins about how working together professionally as director and star would impact their personal relationship. Sarandon, having experienced this on two films while maintaining a personal relationship with Louis Malle, knew it could very easily turn into a hostile situation in which she could walk off the set in anger but still have to face Robbins when she got home. But after much discussion, the couple agreed that their relationship could survive making this movie.

"We told each other early on that anything that happens during this thing is not real," said Robbins in a *Los Angeles Magazine* interview. "But we also knew that directing a film is not a great aphrodisiac."

Robbins put aside *The Cradle Will Rock* and jumped headlong into writing a first draft script for *Dead Man Walking*. That first draft was completed in two weeks and, as she read, Sarandon saw that playing Sister Helen was going to be one of the toughest acting challenges of her career.

The reason for Sarandon's concern was one of those intangibles that actors often face. In Sarandon's eyes, Sister Helen was a one-note performance in which she recites platitudes and apologies and she leads the audience to the far more interesting actors who populate the film. The actress knew that making Sister Helen more than emotional wallpaper would necessitate that Sarandon marshal all her acting skills.

The first draft script was sent to Sister Helen in the fall of 1994 who, despite never having seen a screenplay before, was able to offer a few insights into the reality of nuns and wrote a few scenes of her own in an attempt to inject some humor into what was admittedly a downbeat story.

Dead Man Walking's star power was enhanced when Sean Penn agreed to portray the role of the death-row killer.

But given the pedigree of the project, *Dead Man Walking* had a hard time finding studio interest. This was due, in large part, to the fact that while the whole issue of the death penalty was a hot topic, it was not necessarily a money-making one. One studio head, who has thankfully remained nameless, liked the idea but suggested a more upbeat ending in which the convicted murderer turned out to be innocent.

Eventually Polygram Films agreed to fund *Dead Man Walking* but at a decidedly reduced budget that forced Robbins to take a major pay cut and much of the cast to work for little more than scale. Sarandon's challenge would be less financial and more method acting. In order to effectively portray Sister Helen, she once again had to put on weight, wear no makeup, and basically appear as unglamorous as possible at all times.

But after having committed herself to *Dead Man Walking*, Sarandon began to get cold feet as the start date on the film neared. The culprit was her second thoughts about working with Robbins. "I almost dropped out because I wasn't sure that we could do it together and not kill each other." Sarandon ultimately decided that the possibilities of the film were too great not to take the chance.

By the time *Dead Man Walking* was nearing its start date, it had been officially announced that Sarandon's performance in *The Client* had indeed resulted in her fourth Oscar nomination. Sarandon and Robbins had a good laugh at the prospect of returning, literally, to the scene of the crime and saw the irony in the nomination and the fact that, following their initial anger, the Academy hierarchy had become very conciliatory. Yet, on Oscar night, she once again went away empty-handed.

Dead Man Walking would prove that rare logistical problem for Sarandon and Robbins. The schedule required them to shoot out of state during a time when Eva was still in school. The two youngest children were particularly unhappy at being taken away from home but were placated when Sarandon bought some ducks and set them up in the hotel room bathtub.

Filming began on *Dead Man Walking* in Louisiana's Angola State Prison and later moved to a New York City soundstage. From the beginning the production was overflowing with emotional tensions.

Eighteen-hour days inside the claustrophobic confines of the prison were the norm. Exhaustion was a constant companion. There were occasional equipment problems and the budget was a nagging obstacle. Penn, a talented but volatile actor, was responding to the character and the tone of the film with a festering, angry method approach that was making being around the actor uncomfortable both on and off the set.

The real life of a prison was also a constant companion while they were shooting at Angola State Prison. A death-row inmate was executed at Angola and, as part of a vigil at the prison, Sarandon and Robbins saw firsthand the reality of an execution and its impact on all involved in the process. During filming, a second condemned prisoner was given a last-minute reprieve. Sarandon would later tearfully recall that the prisoner would later be executed.

Sarandon was also going through inner turmoil. Playing a nun, not too long after playing mothers in back-to-back films, she saw the door closing on a career that, to that point, had been built on smoldering sexuality.

"I've gone all the way to the other end of the sexual spectrum," she remembered of that time. "I hope I can come back."

The result was that tensions between Sarandon and Robbins were a constant element of the production. But a lot of those tensions were par for the course on any movie set and that Robbins, because of the long hours, often stayed in a separate room when he was directing. At one point, midway through filming, the couple agreed to live in separate apartments.

"We're not stupid, you know," said Sarandon in *Entertainment Weekly* when discussing those dark days on the set. "It was clear it was going to be different. We definitely had those days when tensions were high. I'm out there working unadorned without lipstick or mascara. So I definitely had moments when I wasn't particularly tactful in terms of trying to figure out what I was doing."

But Sarandon's insistence that she remembered the troubles clearly but did not want to talk about it and Robbins's cryptic, "It was a nightmare but I'm not going to talk about it" only added fuel to the rumors that while *Dead Man Walking* was turning out to be a powerful, unflinching look at the death penalty, it was doing potentially irreparable damage to the couple's eight-year relationship.

But these reports of their personal relationship reportedly unraveling during the making of the film were more than balanced by numerous cast and crew reports that Robbins and Sarandon were running "a nurturing and healthy set." Actor Raymond J. Barry, who had discovered what a hellish shoot can be on the set of Oliver Stone's *Born on the Fourth of July*, praised Sarandon and Robbins's demeanor when he said, "On this, it wasn't the usual bullshit and that had to do with Tim and Susan."

Sarandon looked back on *Dead Man Walking* as one of her toughest acting challenges because most of the acting between Penn and Sarandon was done in scenes in which they were separated by a glass partition. Sarandon ultimately looked on the film as an exercise in which she had no props to work with, was not allowed to touch her acting partner, and could not be in the same room with him. Sarandon surmised that having all those limitations made the acting connection more intimate and pure.

Needless to say, Sarandon and Robbins were eager to promote *Dead Man Walking* and, in the process of meeting with the press, her candor on the often difficult nature of the shoot inadvertently fueled the speculation that the couple's relationship was indeed in trouble. According to a *Los Angeles Times* article, she reportedly told one reporter, "We had four to six days where we really couldn't stand each other." She also reported that, "There are days I hate the way he eats his cereal."

What upset Sarandon when she would read these comments and others is that they were totally taken out of context. When she said them, they were part and parcel of

185

the filmmaking process. When they appeared in print, and decidedly out of context, it appeared that Sarandon was complaining about her personal life with Robbins.

Sarandon later admitted that her remarks "made things difficult" at home for a while and led her to a change of heart regarding her frankness in dealing with the press. "I'm not gonna talk about my personal relationship anymore, except in a generalized, philosophical way."

Which on the surface would appear to be a difficult task. Because Sarandon's nonfilm life is so much a part of who she is, the questions would inevitably cross over into that personal area. And depending on how the actress was feeling on a particular day, she would either go back on her promise and give some tantalizing glimpses into her home life or completely shut down on the subject. But when she did talk, it was obviously from a sense of security that her real life was in a good place.

Dead Man Walking provided a psychological and emotional break with her self-image as an actress and, more importantly, as a woman. During the making of the film, Sarandon felt naked without makeup and would not look at dailies, lest her self-image of a liberated middle-aged woman be damaged. But now she had no choice. And while she felt "devastated" the first couple of times she saw the film, she felt the process had, in a positive sense, purged her of any sense of vanity. Although, in the next breath, she jokingly exclaimed, "Next time, I want to try and get some mascara on."

Dead Man Walking opened to rave reviews and solid

box office. The fear that such a downbeat movie would be box office poison faded away as *Dead Man Walking* did steady business that ultimately saw the movie topping the $100 million mark.

Critics applauded the film as a triumph of filmmaking and of social conscience and it came as no surprise that the Academy Awards were all over the film. Sarandon received her fifth Best Actress nod, Penn a Best Actor nomination, and Robbins a Best Director vote. There was the expected media push and a groundswell of support for the film and, in particular, for Sarandon. If nothing else, the public was itching for another showdown between Sarandon and the Academy.

Sarandon's continued rejection at Oscar time had resulted in the actress not being too excited at her fifth nomination. Robbins had to agree that the prospects for Sarandon seemed dim.

"Susan deserves the Oscar this year," he told the *Calgary Sun*. "But her acting is far too subtle and the two of us are far too political for her to receive her due."

But with the growing feeling that the fifth time might be the charm, Sarandon was suddenly anxious at her chances.

"I'm very good at losing," she joked to *Entertainment Weekly*. "The thing I'm not used to is winning. For me, the fear is having to get out of my seat."

c h a p t e r   e i g h t
"I'M A DESIGNATED HITTER FOR OLDER OVARIES"

Sarandon did get out of her seat on Oscar night, ending her own personal Academy Awards drought, and, in the process, solidified her reputation as the leading light among Hollywood's more mature actresses.

To say that the moment was bittersweet was an understatement. The occasion of Oscar night, personally and professionally, had seen a wide array of emotion expressed over the years. There was the irony that many of those applauding her this night had, literally and figuratively, turned their back on her three years earlier. She had been here before, seemingly assured of an earlier victory, only to come away empty-handed. But this night was a night of triumph.

The media's hope for an angry political diatribe from Sarandon was not realized. One need only look at the smile as she accepted the award to know that Sarandon was nothing if not grateful.

Sarandon's presence in the spotlight, looking positively ravishing, continued to put the lie to the fact that over-

SUSAN SARANDON

forty sexuality was a myth, particularly in Hollywood where over forty for an actress often meant the end of a glamorous career.

Much had been made of Sarandon's sexuality in recent years. To many it was more about her intellect and attitude than any overt physical beauty despite the fact that Sarandon had, quite naturally, matured into a physically enticing person. Sarandon continued to be amused at her portrayal as an aging sex symbol and was clueless as to what it all meant.

"I can't figure out what translates as sensual or sexual except that I think it's something that you feel," she told the *Milwaukee Journal*.

While she would stop short of admitting that she was now the poster woman for middle-age sexuality, the reality was that Sarandon's rise to prominence on a number of professional, political, and social fronts had coincided with the acknowledgment by the popular media that actresses were not only getting older but better . . . sexually. And in the flood of articles and think pieces that were coming out on this new "hot topic," Sarandon's name was often mentioned as the prime example of the attractive older woman, a combination of physical beauty and unbridled intellect.

Following the success of *Dead Man Walking*, the consensus was that Sarandon would be inundated with quality scripts. But while her stock had dramatically risen and she was now regularly getting Hollywood's A offerings, she was, for a time, turning up her nose at everything offered her—and not because the scripts and the characters were inherently bad.

190

It was that she was not interested in playing the flaw-less, automatic heroes who held little tension or interest. And, most likely as a lingering fallout from *Thelma & Louise*, she was not interested in anything that projected even the hint of a positive correlation between sex and violence. Stories that reinforced stereotypes about women, especially pointless exercises about women as victims, were also rejected out of hand. Nor was she inter-ested in the easy out of playing another socially conscious or activist role unless the story was extraordinary.

Sarandon's requirements remained fairly simple. Give her a character with some semblance of dignity and who goes through some kind of believable change and she would be there. But since those kinds of roles were not forthcoming, Sarandon simply decided not to work. Or at least not in the normal, mainstream projects.

Sarandon decided to turn her attention to her political and social side and lend her talents, usually at little or no pay, to projects that appealed to her ideals. She consented to be interviewed for the documentary *The Celluloid Closet*, which took a historical look at the way Hollywood has portrayed homosexuality. She narrated a documen-tary taking a close look at American journalism in *Tell the Truth and Run: George Seldes and the American Press* and performed similar duties in the documentary *Father Roy: Inside the School of Assassins*, an exposé of how the United States government is secretly subverting democ-racy in Central American countries.

More for her amusement and that of her family, Sarandon

also ventured into the world of animation, doing the voice of Bart's ballet teacher in an episode of *The Simpsons*.

In her activist role, Sarandon not too surprisingly chose to stay away from the upcoming presidential campaigns. Still angry at Clinton's patronizing but empty actions regarding human rights and considering his opponent, Bob Dole, a right-wing joke, she chose to stay in the background while many Hollywood bigwigs weighed in on one side or the other. Instead, she put much of her efforts in the direction of helping local, low-profile organizations.

Sarandon had always gravitated to those organizations and people who had no voice and were more grassroots and a little more dangerous than established charities. To her way of thinking, Sarandon was taking care of the groups that nobody else was taking care of.

AIDS-related causes continued to be high on Sarandon's list of good works. These included Housing Works, which provides housing and services for homeless people with AIDS and HIV, and the People with AIDS Coalition, which runs a number of hotlines. Sarandon has often reflected on the fact that her early involvement in AIDS and the fact that so many people were dying in isolation and amid total ignorance on the subject solidified her commitment to AIDS charities.

Her association with We Can, one of her longest ongoing ventures, continued to be more than the expected celebrity lip service. When she was not lobbying the news media and making personal donations to the homeless and poor recycling program, she has served as a founding member of the board.

"She's always there when we need her," said We Can executive director Guy Polhemus in 1998. "She will always come give us a hand at the last minute if she's available."

When it came to espousing a favorite cause, Sarandon would leap at any opportunity to exploit the media, even if it meant going on the slow-witted *Rosie O'Donnell Show*. On that occasion, Sarandon showed up on the softball gabfest with a llama to help publicize the Heifer Project, an organization that provides food and income-producing animals and education to farms and farming communities throughout the world. While many observers saw humor in Sarandon's appearance, the actress insisted that, while the Heifer Project was not what most would consider a glamour charity, it was a very real cause that needed to be addressed.

As was often the case, Sarandon's earnestness often carried the day with perceived fringe organizations like the Heifer Project. She could quote you chapter and verse and make her cause seem viable no matter how unimportant it appeared. Interest in the Heifer Project increased perceptively after Sarandon's appearance on the *Rosie O'Donnell Show* and pointed out how savvy the actress had become in manipulating the media for her purposes.

Sarandon's activist bent had long been the subject of both support and derision. To many talk-show hosts, she was constant fodder for often tasteless and witless jokes or diatribes against more liberal factions while liberals hailed her as a powerful advocate in innumerable causes. Sarandon ignored the former and, in a sense, shied away from the latter. She knew she had some clout but preferred to paint herself as simply one person with an opinion.

Much of her activism now stemmed from the fact that her children and their world were now being affected by many of the problems in the world. By the mid-nineties, one would have to look long and hard to come up with a more perfect amalgamation of actress and activist than Susan Sarandon was presenting to the world.

Not surprisingly, Sarandon was uncomfortable with the notion that she was being painted as some kind of Mother Teresa and would often have a good laugh at the image of her as some kind of all-purpose activist. In fact, Sarandon is quick to point out the very ordinary nature of her life, at least on a personal front, who, because of her celebrity, is in a position to put her time to good use on behalf of causes.

"I think everyone is supposed to be a protagonist in his or her own life," she has said. "You have to watch out for what's happening on your school board, complain when your air is being polluted, and defend your First Amendment rights when they're challenged."

On another front, Sarandon continued to search out the most challenging acting roles possible and found a rather offbeat one, considering her past credits, in the voice of the character Spider in the live-action animated feature *James and the Giant Peach*. Sarandon had narrated her share of documentaries of late and had admittedly had a good time doing *The Simpsons*. But the notion of showing up on an isolated soundstage to add dialogue to a total fantasy creation continued to appeal to her. And again, her decision to a degree was based on family in that she was finally doing a film that she would feel comfortable letting her children see.

Sarandon's concession to the needs and desires of her children, even on this seemingly minor level, had been part of the growth process for the actress. Giving over so much of herself to her children after so many years of admitted self-involvement had been cathartic as well as a loving rite of passage. The result was a family that was surprisingly well-rounded and one that did not suffer from having parents of privilege. The children had a clear vision of who their parents were and what their circumstances were. From the moment she could comprehend such matters, Eva had been made perfectly aware of her parents' history together. That Robbins and Sarandon were not legally married was never a deep, dark secret to any of their children. Sarandon's philosophy of total honesty had produced three exceedingly normal children.

Her interest in the growing division between rich and poor and how it impacted on law enforcement led Sarandon to be involved in the 1997 documentary *187: Documented*, which focused on big-city police forces and their treatment of minorities.

Sarandon's forays into nonmainstream ventures in 1996 and 1997 predictably shut her out of serious Oscar consideration. While the critics once again offered up the actress as an example of somebody whose independent approach to her career had potentially short-circuited her artistry, Sarandon could not have cared less.

"I think life is so much bigger than my craft that I

would rather invest my genius in my life. It has many more challenges, many more surprises. It may even demand more from the imagination."

Sarandon moved back into a more traditional film in *Twilight*, a small film noir-style murder mystery centering on three past-their-prime individuals. Despite the film's modest intent, it did attract the attention of superstar actors Paul Newman and Gene Hackman who, along with Sarandon, saw potential in the quiet elegance of three characters in the twilight of their lives dealing with the consequences of the past and present.

Sarandon's role of a movie star who had seen better days must have seemed ironic to the actress who, at a point when her cinematic counterpart was in decline, was enjoying a totally unexpected career jump into that rar-efied strata of stardom. Sarandon saw through the slight murder mystery to the story's core and immediately jumped at the opportunity. In the aftermath of *Dead Man Walking*, she embraced the opportunity to dirty up her screen image and, after what seemed like an eternity, to once again wear sexy clothes and makeup.

Twilight was a platter of delights for the discerning filmgoer. The sexual attraction between Sarandon and Newman generated some legitimate tension in both a physical and emotional sense. In oh-so-subtle ways, the audience had the opportunity to see how sly and duplici-tous evil can play out in the hands of a veteran actress. In a sense, *Twilight* was Sarandon's answer to the notion of getting older and getting better.

Good reviews on *Twilight* reflected the chance she took in the film. *Commonweal* offered, "Sarandon does the femme fatale number to perfection and even humanizes it enough to convince us that such a woman is capable of her own version of fidelity." An insightful review in the *National Review* said, "She is earthily feminine but with a hint of hidden fragility."

Twilight, despite being only a moderate success at the box office, proved to be a pure acting exercise for Sarandon. It gave her some solid screen time with the legend Newman and it added fuel to the idea that Sarandon, now perilously close to fifty, had defied the odds and the public's perception of sexuality as the domain of the young to revolutionize the cause of women in middle age. Sarandon remained suitably humble.

"I don't mind getting older. I thank God for my health, for my stamina and my work which is getting better all the time. I've hit my stride."

In dissecting Sarandon's career into the late nineties, it becomes apparent that the actress has not always been one to either capitalize on her successes or, for that matter, to play it safe. Wiser choices in the wake of *Pretty Baby* and *Atlantic City* most likely would have made Sarandon a household name by the early eighties. The same case could be made for the erratic follow-ups to her other great moments, *Bull Durham* and *Dead Man Walking*. But upon closer examination, one finds that Susan Sarandon's choices have not been all that different from all the other reigning stars of Hollywood. The reality of having to make a living and the desire to work has often found big stars making less than ideal choices. Sarandon has been no exception.

In March 1998, Sarandon's long and often maligned commitment to causes was rewarded when ShowWest, an organization of movie-house owners, awarded Sarandon its annual Humanitarian of the Year Award. The award was important to Sarandon in a way that her Oscar win could not touch. She was gratified for the award but claimed that it was more important in bringing much-needed attention to the many organizations she was supporting. And, in accepting the accolades for her good works, she once again acknowledged the importance of her family in the things she does.

"I see how my life and the lives of my kids are connected to the outside world. How can you not participate in the very world you live?"

chapter   nine

"AM I GOING TO SHUT UP? NO"

Sarandon going topless at age fifty-one? It was a novel notion, one that would seem to bring the image of Susan Sarandon as poster woman for grown-up sexuality logically to the forefront.

It was an idea that the actress had long entertained over the years and had skillfully avoided. *Playboy* reportedly had been after the actress to bare all in a tasteful pictorial for years. There had been those moments, such as in *White Palace*, where she teased with her physical beauty and sexuality but, even in that context, it was within an overtly erotic concept. For Sarandon to even consider baring all at this point, especially as it pertained to the sensibilities of her children, the circumstances would have to be exceptional.

Which is why her choosing to appear topless in *Illuminata* seemed an odd but not unexpected Sarandon choice. *Illuminata*, a small art-house film that chronicled the struggles of a small theater troupe at the turn of the century, came and went fairly quickly in August 1998. However, the film was distinguished by solid ensemble acting and showed Sarandon in her acting element as a maturing diva. Sarandon laughingly agreed with the opinion that she was, in essence, playing herself and that the role was an example of how she had turned her natural-aging process into something constructive.

A smattering of mixed reviews tended to pick up on that fact. *Variety* said, "Sarandon is beautiful as the aging, amoral diva."

By the late nineties, however, the small, quirky films like *Illuminata* were becoming more of a lark for Sarandon, the reason being that mainstream Hollywood was finally coming closer to identifying with the actress's sensibility and was making commercial films that offered more challenging roles, the kind that Sarandon was gravitating to now well into her fifties.

For many longtime observers of Sarandon's career, there were the shudders of disappointment that the actress was now settling for safer choices in the face of bigger paychecks. But the argument could be made, and Sarandon herself often made it, that she was simply doing the work that interested her and that selling out was not in her vocabulary.

Her next film, the very mainstream-commercially savvy *Stepmom*, which paired her with Julia Roberts and Ed Harris, succeeded in showcasing yet another emerging element of the Sarandon palette of styles and colors. Essentially a big-budget tearjerker in which a woman loses her husband to a younger woman and finds her misfortune compounded when she is diagnosed with terminal cancer,

Sarandon saw the film as an opportunity to turn the dying-parent cliché on its head with a portrait that was more life-affirming and defiant than sad and weepy.

Sarandon, who was executive-producing, for the first time since *The Great Smokey Roadblock* had to be in the forefront of big-studio politics, whereas she had only been on the receiving end of it in the past.

She felt herself a perfect fit, temperamentally and creatively, with costar and coproducer Roberts, a close friend since they had rubbed shoulders in *The Player*. Many even saw Roberts as a glamorous nineties version of Sarandon. Choosing director Chris Columbus brought her into the often volatile meetings and deals that are the lifeblood of Hollywood. Now that she was in the position to speak out and have people listen, she took every opportunity to mold the *Stepmom* story to her tastes. The script was rewritten several times and there was some concern, mostly from those outside the production, that Sarandon and Roberts would not get along. Sarandon was amused at this almost stereotypical perception.

"If you make a movie with a male star, everyone assumes you're fucking," laughed Sarandon at the primarily press-generated feud. "If it's a female star, everyone assumes you're fighting."

But ultimately the opposite was true. The chemistry between the pair was very good and it resulted in a strong onscreen give-and-take whenever the two actresses shared the camera. But Roberts recalled in an interview with the *Calgary Sun* that friendship essentially went out the window when it was time to roll film and that she often felt intimidated by Sarandon the actress.

"We really worked to create those strong, volatile elements between those two people," she said. "There were times when Susan would walk off the set and I'd say, 'A little too good, just a little too good.' She's this great force and this great presence. You sort of want to work that much more cleverly or interestingly because this is a friend. The first day we got there (to the set), I thought, 'Wow! If she thinks I'm bad. . . .' "

But while Sarandon was coming across, at least to Roberts, as together, in actuality the part was not easy on Sarandon's vanity and ego. Because of the nature of the piece, Sarandon had to come across as frumpy and terminal while Roberts played her younger woman with lots of glitz. The contrast was obvious and Sarandon had to dig deep to keep her ego in check.

"You have to strip away everything," said Sarandon of her *Stepmom* experience, "and find some inner glow."

Sarandon's performance, earthy and restrained in a very mannered way, easily raised the bar of *Stepmom* above the expected sentimentality to something very real world in tone. In a way, Sarandon turned in an ironically old-school performance at a time when she was coming to grips with roles she had spent a long time avoiding. *Stepmom* added fuel to Sarandon's long-held conviction that her best roles were still ahead of her.

Earthly Possessions, based on the Anne Tyler novel, continued the procession of exemplary roles that seemed to fall quite naturally into Sarandon's lap. In this made-for-cable feature, Sarandon played a disillusioned housewife who is taken hostage by an inept young bank robber. In yet another effective take on the older woman-younger man relationship, the center piece of *Earthly Possessions* finds the two desperate people living, learning, and loving each other in ways that run much deeper than the expected exploitive elements and results, much to Sarandon's praise, in the two people believably emerging from this experience as better people.

Sarandon, however, was very much the chameleon of the piece; quietly going about the business of transforming her character from insecure and burned out to confident and hopeful in a manner that exuded the actress's obvious strengths as a wise and polished performer.

Actor Stephen Dorff recalled that, much like the experiences of others who had worked with Sarandon, he believed he was sitting at the feet of a true genius during the making of *Earthly Possessions*.

"I just followed Susan," he told a reporter. "Whatever she did, I did. I trusted Susan."

When not working in front of the camera, the actress's interest in political and social causes, both big and small, continued to brand her as a voice of reason. In April 1999, Sarandon returned to her hometown to read to local children as part of the national day of enlightenment by the organization Read Across America. The same month Sarandon was spotted manning a carnival booth as part of a street fair sponsored by the Elizabeth Glaser Pediatric

AIDS Foundation. The month of April also saw Sarandon presented with the first annual Raul Julia Global Citizen Award for her contributions to ending world hunger.

Sarandon had not given up on her more revolutionary, in-your-face tendencies. In March of 1999, Sarandon was linking arms and providing fiery rhetoric in response to the aggressive police tactics by the New York City police that resulted in the death of recent immigrant Amadou Diallo. That day, 219 demonstrators were arrested, including Sarandon. As the police moved in and snapped the cuffs on her, Sarandon was heard to exclaim, "If we're not here, we're saying what happened is acceptable and normal and I think that does a disservice to others. Everything we can do to keep this issue alive is really important."

In the meantime, Tim Robbins's growing reputation as a writer-director on *Dead Man Walking* and, to a lesser degree, *Bob Roberts*, finally led to his getting the necessary financing to revive his long-dormant *Cradle Will Rock*, his quasi-fictional account of a federally funded Depression-era theater company which clashes with the U.S. government over charges that a production is propagating left-wing propaganda. Needless to say, the relation between Sarandon and Robbins on this film was a lot less tense than when they shot *Dead Man Walking*.

Sarandon, despite playing the less politically centered role of duplicitous Margherita Sarfetti, was keenly aware of the political ramifications of her partner's film and the ongoing clashes between art, politics, and the ever-present specter of censorship.

Sarandon had always found herself interested in the fact that the public seemed to feel artists should not be politically or socially involved on the grounds that every work of art establishes its own set of values. It was a notion that the actress did not agree with.

Cradle Will Rock also appealed to Sarandon on a number of creative levels. "As a woman, you hardly ever get to work with women. I was jazzed. Ensembles are so much fun. You don't have that burden you have when you're carrying a movie, to be in every scene. I don't get to play bad guys too often. I like the director's work. I like him. And I thought it would be a fun part to do."

Sarandon as artist was well on the way to establishing a heretofore unexplored element of her craft in the film *Anywhere But Here*, in which a desperate and totally unsympathetic mother takes her straightlaced daughter, portrayed by Natalie Portman, away from her conservative Midwest surroundings and off to Hollywood in a hare-brained scheme to make her daughter into a movie star.

Esthetically the film was an opportunity for the actress to get back into "the makeup and eyeliner" type of roles she was noted for early in her career. Creatively, it was a light-year stretch in which for her character to succeed, Adele August had to be totally unsympathetic and risk clouding Hollywood's by now fairly clear perception of the actress.

But Sarandon liked the idea so much that she had kept an eye on the script for nearly a decade as it went through the numerous rewrites and delays that characterize development hell. There was also the matter of timing. When

SUSAN SARANDON

Anywhere But Here first made the studio rounds in 1990, movies starring two women were considered death at the box office. Buddy movies were about men, not women. But, as Sarandon is fond of noting, *Thelma & Louise* changed all that and made *Anywhere But Here* possible.

Now that it was finally about to happen, the consensus was that Sarandon was about to make a big mistake, thanks, in large part, to the latest round of Sarandon type-casting. Winning the Oscar for *Dead Man Walking* had turned into a double-edged sword. It had given legitimacy to a long-unappreciated career. But from studio heads to directors to audiences to reviewers, it had shut the door on Sarandon seemingly ever doing another lighthearted role. She was now "THE SERIOUS ACTRESS."

Many in Sarandon's circle of supporters did not take kindly to the character in *Anywhere But Here* and were blunt in their assessment that Sarandon would be making a mistake by taking the role.

But Sarandon reasoned that, as her daughter, Eva, was about to turn fourteen, the same age as the daughter in the film, she felt it would be a good opportunity to practice "before the crisis is actually in your house."

Director Wayne Wang, in an *Empire* interview, was enthusiastic in his wanting Sarandon in the film.

"I thought she had a lot of credit in the bank for what she's done," said Wang. "It was good for this role because it's sometimes a little brash and crazy and unsympathetic. She took some risks doing this. I was definitely interested in playing around with her screen history."

Given her star billing, Sarandon was integral to the preparation of the film. She was one of those who suggested a more subtle approach to a sex scene in the original script that, because of the actress's attitude toward onscreen nudity, would have forced Natalie Portman out of the film. And it was at her insistence that Portman was cast as her daughter. She had admired Portman's humor and strength in previous films but it was her natural grace, much like the way Sarandon approached her roles, that turned the tide in her favor. Sarandon's instincts were good as *Anywhere But Here* benefited from what turned out to be a situation of mutual respect in which Sarandon admitted learning as much from the younger woman as Portman undoubtedly learned from Sarandon.

Despite a mixed critical reception to the film, *Anywhere But Here* offered up an evenhanded, if often critical, look at Sarandon's performance. *Variety* stated, "Sarandon's acting gets more multishaded and refined in the last reel." The *Los Angeles Times* critiqued, "Sarandon and Mona Simpson's character do not make a good fit." *New Times* acknowledged, "Rather than developing a contradictory or layered character, Sarandon is allowed to be only one adjective at a time." The *New York Times* praised, "It's a pleasure, if not a surprise, to find Susan Sarandon so showstopping."

Rather than run from this recent offering of mother roles, Sarandon was actively embracing the notion of reinventing the perception of motherhood in all its many facets. Not surprisingly she saw playing mothers as being a creative and social challenge.

"No one's tapped into this category because of the taboo," she explained. "Most of the mothers we've seen on the screen have been one-dimensional, sappy, stand by your man moms. Once you crossed that line, there was no turning back."

And Sarandon was more than willing to take motherhood into the final frontier as she explained in a *Washington Post* interview about her own perception of cinematic, flawed motherhood. "Let's get real. It has to be real life. The audience can appreciate that there's no clear heroine and bad guy. I fought very hard for that [especially in *Stepmom*]. It would have been a different movie if it had just been me falling apart."

Sarandon's professional workload continued to stray from predictable choices in the coming months. She took a minor and largely uncredited part as the animated voice of Mrs. Clarke in the direct-to-video children's feature *Our Friend Martin*, a story inspired by the life of Martin Luther King Jr. In the art-house film *Joe Gould's Secret*, a largely biographical story of the relationship between a *New Yorker* writer and a 1940s street person, she played the part of a publisher named Alice Neel.

Neither role was likely to earn her much fanfare and, in fact, *Our Friend Martin* does not show up on most of Sarandon's filmography lists. But Sarandon was, at that point, not looking for any great challenges. She was looking to work with good people (in the case of *Joe Gould's Secret,* director Stanley Tucci and actor Ian Holm) and basically take it easy.

Sarandon had often proven that she would go to any

length to help support a worthy cause. One of the oddest came in 1999 when *Marie Claire* magazine agreed to donate farm animals to the Heifer Project International if she would pull off eighteen unusual stunts in public. One of the toughest had the actress walking into a Manhattan diner, grabbing a stranger's sandwich, and biting into it.

"I was terrified in the beginning and then this guy shared his sandwich with me, without recognizing me, and I thought New York is so crazy, this might actually be fun."

Other tasks completed included convincing a jogger to eat a Twinkie, persuading a group of stock traders to hold hands on Wall Street, and to ask employees at the Gap stores for the Monica Lewinsky dress. The only task she failed at was convincing a patron at a strip club to call his wife. Instead, Sarandon received a lap dance from one of the dancers. Once she got over the shock, all she could ask the dancer was if she had to declare tips to the IRS.

Throughout the summer and fall of 1999, Sarandon was once again active on the political front. She was involved in the plight of the Kosovo refugees who were mired in a political quagmire that was keeping thousands of families in refugee camps and, in many cases, separated from other family members. Sarandon helped raise funds for food and shelter and, as part of the entertainment-based group Film Aid, helped secure funds for projectors, VCRs, and other equipment to show films and educational programming at the camps.

Sarandon once again took to the streets of New York in October 1999 when Mayor Rudy Giuliani attempted to cut off museum funding for the Brooklyn Museum of Art when the museum refused to close down the controversial art exhibition "Sensations." For Sarandon, a proud, lifelong New Yorker, the issue struck particularly close to home. Memories of her early involvement in the Creative Coalition and her testifying on behalf of the National Endowment for the Arts in Congress came flooding back.

She was one of the featured speakers at a protest rally on the steps of the Brooklyn Museum that seemed like a three-ring circus. Animal-rights activists were protesting displays of dead animals and antiexhibit members of the religious right were handing out vomit bags to those about to enter the exhibit. Amid the chaos, Sarandon's voice was heard loud and clear.

"I find it shocking that this mayor's challenges to the First Amendment are constant. This is a city whose selling power is that it's where an exchange of free ideas started. You don't have to like the exhibit but you certainly don't censor it. Let intelligent people make up their own minds."

Giuliani, who at that time was right in the middle of a hotly contested Senate race, was incensed that the museum controversy was putting a blight on his bid for higher office and was particularly irritated that Sarandon, somebody who was guaranteed to draw the media spotlight, was at the forefront of the opposition. In fact, Giuliani began to take great pains to avoid Sarandon and, in one instance, canceled an appearance when he discovered that Sarandon might be there.

Sarandon's continued efforts on behalf of AIDS-HIV

and hunger relief were rewarded in September 1999 when she was honored with the Amnesty International Media Spotlight Award. In accepting the award, Sarandon once more took the opportunity to call to the attention of people that there was still a lot of work to be done and that they could all make a difference by getting involved.

That Sarandon's life would be of any historical significance was always a laughable concept for the actress. And so she was surprised when the popular Arts and Entertainment Channel disclosed that they were working on a profile of the actress for their highly rated *Biography* series. As the airdate for the biography approached, she assumed the entire family would be present at its premiere airing. But, as Sarandon recalled in a *Calgary Sun* interview, Robbins and their children were less than enthusiastic.

Her family suggested that she tape it so that they could watch it when there was nothing better on television. Sarandon was legitimately hurt by her family's lack of interest.

Sarandon ended up watching her life unfold alone on a tiny TV screen. And her feeling about the way her life was portrayed was less than enthusiastic.

"I thought it was a pretty boring life. It was much more difficult living it. They're not going to get your life in forty-five minutes. But at least it didn't insult or offend anyone in my family. It was a bit of a jolt because it forced me to look back at my life."

But Sarandon was quick to point out to the *Calgary Sun* that her discomfort with watching her life unfold did not in any way mean that she was not content with where her odyssey had brought her.

"I have it all. My children are bright. I have a man who continues to make me laugh and I get plenty [of money] to do what I love."

As 1999 drew to a close, Sarandon once again turned her attention to national politics and particularly the upcoming presidential election. That the Republicans were looking to run a second generation of Bush (George W.) was of particular concern to Sarandon, who was often fond of repeating a phrase regularly used during one of his many campaign speaches by activist and future presidential candidate Ralph Nader, who once described Bush "as a corporation running for president disguised as a person." And, despite being a card-carrying liberal, she continued to find fault with the Democratic Party. "The Democratic Party has not been giving me, or half the Americans who do not go to the polls, anything."

Sarandon had a good laugh at the wide variety of splinter candidates that were publicly announcing, often with tongue firmly planted in cheek, that they too were throwing their hats into the presidential ring. She jokingly suggested that Warren Beatty and Oprah Winfrey would be the ideal choices because they were so rich that they would not need any outside money to mount a successful campaign. But Sarandon eventually stopped joking. For the actress this was serious business.

She considered the fact that the two major political parties were merely puppets at the beck and call of corporate America to be an insult to the people who actually cared about democracy. The easy way out would have been to just not vote and to advise others to do the same. But that was not her style. Her instincts were to get down in the trenches and support a candidate who was not bought and paid for and who had what she believed to be the best interests of real people at heart. She did not want to waste her vote.

Sarandon began looking around for an alternate choice.

chapter   ten

"ANYBODY WHO VOTES SHOULD VOTE WITH THEIR HEART"

I n Ralph Nader Sarandon felt she had found her ideal
candidate.

Nader, a long-standing political maverick who had
spent years using facts and logic to hold the feet of both
political parties to the fire, had in recent years turned his
attention to environmental and global concerns under the
banner of the Green Party. With the growing dissatisfaction with the two main political wings and the growing
popularity in recent elections of viable third-party candidates, Nader in 1999 announced his candidacy for president in the 2000 election on the Green Party ticket. His
platform would encompass such liberal concerns as public
and private financing of political campaigns and tougher
penalties for corporate crime.

All of this appealed to Sarandon, Robbins, and a
growing number of politically astute young people who
were looking for any excuse to return to the political
process that they had long ago abandoned. Sarandon was
particularly frustrated at the prospect of having to endure

another Bush in the White House and the very real threat of censorship such a presidency would no doubt entail.

As was her custom, Sarandon did her homework. She discovered that Nader had always been consistent when it came to issues of the environment and had gone on record seemingly forever in attacking the corporate influence in Washington. Satisfied that this was a man of conscience and integrity, Sarandon wasted little time in getting behind Nader.

"I'm just so tired of voting from a place of fear," she said in announcing her support for Nader. "When this man [Nader] said he would do it, I said, 'If there's a time for change it's now.'"

Sarandon was paying a lot more than lip service to Nader's campaign. She studied up on the issues and when she chose to speak at rallies or record telephone messages on his behalf, they were laced with Sarandon's agreeable blend of quiet passion and nuts-and-bolts logic, heavy on the statistics and figures that she felt were conspicuously absent from the messages of the Democratic and Republican Parties.

And through her intense scrutiny of what an admittedly long-shot Nader presidency might accomplish, Sarandon became aware that, despite all the rhetoric that conventional politics was inclusive of all socioeconomic strata, the reality was that America in the year 2000 was very much a class-divided society in which corporate America was the puppeteer pulling the strings.

This hit Sarandon very hard for while she was living

comfortably in a state of upper-class celebrity, her heart and soul had remained very much of the street, believing in the power of grassroots movements to bring about change. Sarandon once again found herself politically energized and ready to do battle.

Sarandon's stepping forward for what many political traditionalists considered a disruptive, fringe candidate drew the ire of many observers of the political and Hollywood scene. There were some rumbles, although not as many as in years gone by, that Sarandon's involvement would hurt her standing in Hollywood, especially if a conservative candidate did win the White House. Others warned that Sarandon's involvement might swing a close election into the hands of a far-right candidate, as many political pundits considered Bush to be.

And once again these pundits missed the point. Sarandon was not in this to wield power and to become an influence broker. She had her issues and was only looking for the right person to deal with them.

She was particularly attuned to a growing antiglobalization sentiment and looked upon the coming meetings by the industrial powers in Seattle, Washington, and the growing tides of resentment toward impending corporate takeovers on a worldwide basis with interest. When the meetings were disrupted by vocal and often violent protests late in 1999, Sarandon saw it as a call to arms to right the wrongs and to give the power back to the people.

"I think when you've worked a lot of grass roots like I have, you understand that things take a circuitous route.

I think it's time to renew Democracy and take it back and this is the way to do it."

Sarandon was upfront and in the political limelight. But this time, there was no concern that any of her speaking out would hinder her career. Sarandon had gotten too big and too powerful within Hollywood to give the thought of reprisals a thought. Which, as the early weeks and months of 2000 commenced, she was even more vocal and participatory in the things that concerned her.

This was why she willingly lent her time and talents to narrating a portion of a documentary centered around the Seattle demonstrations entitled *This Is What Democracy Looks Like*. The goals of the documentary, to ultimately be screened on college campuses and to be used by grass-roots groups as a fund-raising tool, were modest and in keeping with Sarandon's ideals.

Not that all of Sarandon's sporadic film work in 2000 would be serious stuff. The thought of her family came first in a movie that her young children could see. She agreed to do the voice of the animated character Coco LaBouche in the children's feature-length cartoon *Rugrats in Paris*.

Sarandon chuckled as she recalled the challenge of playing an animated character who, much like the character Cruella De Vil in *101 Dalmations*, spent much of her time screaming. "After about five hours [in the recording studio] my vocal chords were ripped to shreds. But it was also therapeutic because I got rid of all my mean thoughts about little kids who misbehave."

Feeling in a playful mood, Sarandon agreed to appear

as a guest on the critically acclaimed, late-night sketch comedy television series, *Mad TV*. In several hilarious moments on that show, Sarandon took potshots at popular cultural institutions and proved that she had a good sense of humor in skewering her own public persona.

Robbins's film *Cradle Will Rock* finally turned its good notices into a distribution deal and was released in the early months of 2000. Accompanying the film was a hip, largely alternative-rock soundtrack whose highlight was a song entitled "Croon Spoon" which featured a duet between Pearl Jam lead singer Eddie Vedder and Sarandon who, to the surprise of many, showed she could still carry a tune.

As an offshoot of her involvement in children's literacy programs, Sarandon appeared in the HBO special "Goodnight Moon and Other Sleepytime Tales," a children's show about bedtime rituals in which Sarandon told stories and showcased her more motherly side, in direct contrast to her large image as actress-activist.

But, for the most part, Sarandon chose to see in 2001 with a flurry of political and social involvement, for which she received a number of awards that focused on her political and social activism rather than her acting prowess.

In January, Sarandon was voted one of the *Ladies Home Journal*'s "Most Fascinating Women" of 1999. An even more prestigious honor was bestowed upon Sarandon in April when, on the heels of her helping assemble a report on the State of the World's Children 2000, she was appointed a Special Representative of the United Nations Children's Fund (UNICEF). Sarandon was genuinely honored.

"My intent is to speak on behalf of those whose voices are less readily heard, children and women at risk," she said in accepting the honor. "This is just about an extended version of being a mother. If you can just see all the children of the world as your own, all the mothers as you are, we can make a huge difference."

Sarandon continued to be a popular draw on college campuses with a January 2000 appearance at Columbia University, a fine example of Sarandon as raconteur and guiding light. For two hours Sarandon, dressed all in black, entertained students with tales of her childhood, her career, her political views, and her spirituality. And, in the end, she took the opportunity to advise the students to be fearless on their own journeys.

"Plan to be surprised, take a chance, and be open to possibilities," she encouraged the crowd. "Almost everything in my own life has been unplanned. I got here because all the things that were going to happen, didn't happen."

This was a rare admission on Sarandon's part. Having readily admitted over the years that her career and life had not unfolded according to any grand plan, this was a rare moment when she essentially admitted that luck had a lot to do with it and that spirituality, rather than her presumed intelligence and common sense, was her guiding light.

As the year progressed, it seemed that Susan Sarandon was never far away from a good fight, especially if she felt the cause was just. The actress-activist continued to find much to defend on a wide variety of fronts.

She joined a star-studded group of celebrities, scientists, and members of Congress to say that strict federal government guidelines regarding research on the medical benefits of marijuana, even in the face of the Department of Health and Human Services edicts that would ease current marijuana research practices, were blocking research that could potentially benefit millions. And when Paramount Television went ahead with its plans to give notorious radio personality and antigay activist Dr. Laura Schlessinger her own television show, Sarandon added her own voice to the protest when she supplied a message to the Stop Dr. Laura Web site which read, in part, "Dr. Laura has a right to her opinion, but I think it's irresponsible of Paramount to not give equal time, at least, to a person with a more enlightened and contemporary perspective."

And the battles for injustice did not stop there. Many were beginning to see New York City as a place where personal freedoms and questionable police and government tactics were often a common occurrence, literally in Sarandon's own backyard.

Such was the case in April when the city, against vocal opposition from the Puerto Rican and Latino community, sold the El Bohio Community Center, an important deterrent to gang violence in the Puerto Rican community, to a private concern. Sarandon, who had long served on the board of El Bohio, was incensed. Shortly after the sale of the center, Sarandon joined a number of community leaders at a press conference protesting the sale.

In response, the NYPD formed a rolling gate with a patrol car, moving the car back and forth in front of the entrance to the press conference, hindering the entrance to many reporters. For Sarandon, the El Bohio protest was a moral victory. It did not stop the sale but it was, like many of the protests Sarandon had participated in over the years, a positive effort in which the all-important "word" got out.

"You do what you can do," said a somewhat resigned Sarandon in the aftermath of the protest. "You can't live with yourself if you don't. I'm a New Yorker and I'm involved here as a New Yorker."

Sarandon's high degree of philanthropy has continued to be a challenge as the third leg of a triangle that encompasses family and career. She has long maintained a policy of not leaving New York during the school year to work. That edict also stretches to her charitable works.

"I don't do as much as I wish I could," she once sighed. "The amount of things I turn down. . . . You wouldn't believe how many requests I get. It's very heartbreaking that I can't do more."

With the presidential campaign now in full swing, Sarandon was conspicuous by her presence in the Nader campaign, appearing at Green Party rallies and recording phone messages extolling the virtues of Ralph Nader and his economic and social platform. Sarandon also took every opportunity to attack the opposition and, in the case of Republican candidate, George Bush, she found an easy target in the then-Texas governor's pro-death penalty stance and the fact that Texas had the highest execution rate in the United States.

"We stand a chance of getting a president who has probably killed more people before he gets into office than any president in the history of the United States," she said during one fiery speech. "It means you are 'tough on crime.' It means you are for 'law and order.' It means that you are for 'control.' And if you are against the death penalty it seems you are for 'anarchy' and a 'bleeding heart liberal.'"

Midway through 2000, Sarandon, under the auspices of UNICEF, traveled to India and Tanzania to inspect UNICEF-sponsored projects in the regions of Tamil Nadu and Mumbai. She had gone to India in an attempt to educate herself. Like most Americans, India was a mystery to Sarandon. She had heard of the stereotypes, a cross between those engaged in the Kama Sutra and those struggling in the quagmires of the slums. What she found among even the lowest classes of people living amid often squalid conditions was an amazing strength and spirit. But she also found concern in her visit to a center for children of HIV-positive parents and an education facility for young girls who had drifted into the life of the "sex workers," India's thinly veiled version of prostitution.

Likewise, in Tanzania she was alternately encouraged and disheartened as she observed a number of UNICEF-sponsored HIV and AIDS programs struggling against ignorance, prejudice, and underfunding. In one instance, Sarandon recalled having to fight back tears as she met with a woman who had inherited her dead sister's seven children after the woman succumbed to AIDS. During another portion of her Tanzania trip she encountered an elderly woman who was raising her nine grandchildren alone.

Sarandon was touched by the experience. "These women can't fulfill their children's basic needs. Shelter, nutrition, medical care, safety. There's no level on which they're not vulnerable."

Sarandon at a press conference expressed her concern that the specter of AIDS and the plight of uneducated and exploited women was not being addressed with either concern or money. "There isn't enough dialogue. It [HIV] is a subject that still seems to be taboo. The women are isolated and the children are shunned." She further speculated that even if the Indian authorities were acknowledging the extent of the problem, they did not seem to be making the problems a priority.

Sarandon's concern continued once she returned to the United States and reported on her findings to UNICEF. She was passionate in stating that the rights of the children have to be recognized with immediate financial aid to relief and educational programs.

Sarandon was not limiting herself to international issues. Despite a long and often acrimonious relationship with Hollywood, she was, at her core, a dues-paying Screen Actors Guild member and very much pro-union. And so she was more than a little interested when the Screen Actors Guild and the American Federation of Television and Radio Artists struck against the commercial industry for six months over the question of increased residuals for cable and Internet payment. Sarandon and

Robbins were vocal in support of the striking actors and, on a couple of occasions, walked the picket lines in Los Angeles in solidarity with their fellow, often lesser-known actors.

In August, Sarandon took the opportunity to combine business with pleasure when she, Robbins, and their children went to Las Vegas where she met with the press to help promote the premiere of the *Rugrats in Paris*. Their stay in Vegas, Sarandon's very first visit to the gambling mecca, was enjoyable in a Disneyland sort of way. While Sarandon attended to movie business, Tim took Jack and Miles on a very touristy sort of tour of the city and its attractions. Her daughter, Eva, now age fourteen, was allowed to bring along a friend and, surprisingly to onlookers, Sarandon and Robbins got the teenage girls their own room on a different floor.

"I'm not at all that worried," said Sarandon when asked about the degree of freedom she afforded her daughter. "Eva is very responsible for her age. I find the more I treat my children like adults, the more adult they behave."

Sarandon took time off from what was turning into a rush of activist activity in September when she and Robbins traveled to Deauville, France, where Sarandon was the recipient of a Lifetime Achievement Award. Those in attendance were not sure what to expect in Sarandon's acceptance speech. What they got was a highly charged, emotional, and totally politically incorrect attack on America and its restrictive political and social policies.

Once again she attacked presidential candidate George

225

Bush on his death penalty stance, describing the practice as arbitrary, capricious, and racist and a concept that does not work. And, before the assembled world press, she put the blame for a lack of a healthy debate on the death penalty back in the lap of the media. "People unfortunately listen to celebrities more than they do the news. Instead of covering the death penalty they are covering Brad Pitt's wedding and that is the state the U.S. is in now."

She also acknowledged that it took a lot of courage for anyone to speak out against the prevailing U.S. party line. "It's a very reactionary time and there are a lot of civil liberties that are being eroded. People are being frightened and it is not easy to come out against something that makes you seem unsympathetic."

Sarandon plunged back into supporting the third-party candidacy of Ralph Nader. The Nader candidacy was surprising in that it was, unlike previous third-party candidates such as perennial also-ran Pat Buchanan, actually drawing on a sizable, disaffected group of voters. While nobody was giving Nader any real chance of winning the election, it was becoming evident that in this close race the Democrats could be hurt by the number of those normally party loyalists seizing on the Nader candidacy as an alternative to the major political parties as well as a way to vent their frustration.

Sarandon stepped up her participation in the Nader campaign as the election drew closer. She exhorted a packed, star-studded Madison Square Garden fund-raiser to get out the vote. When the two mainstream candidates would not allow Nader to participate in the presidential debates on the grounds that he was not a viable candidate (despite the fact that polls indicated Nader was pulling 6 to 10 percent of the projected vote in a number of states), Sarandon joined Nader and a number of other celebrities in filing a lawsuit in an unsuccessful attempt to get him into the debates.

At a subsequent rally in New York's Washington Square Park Sarandon addressed about two hundred people. There was a sense of disappointment and resignation at Nader's exclusion from the debates and the fact that pollsters were now downsizing Nader's candidacy to a dark-horse status. In her heart, Sarandon knew that the pollsters were right. But, as always, she was looking at the big picture. A sizable showing in the national election would put the Green Party on the map. Whoever did win the presidential election would be in the position of having to reckon with a number of disaffected Americans. For Sarandon, Nader's candidacy was a win-win situation and had been well worth the fight.

And so as she took to the stage, Sarandon was nothing if not energized and passionate in encouraging the assembled crowd to keep the faith and get out the vote.

"I'm happy to finally be voting for someone I believe in," she told them. "I want to vote from my heart. It's up to you to be the apostles. You're the smoking gun."

Whatever views one holds of the 2000 presidential election, Sarandon stayed true to her underlying beliefs despite their unpopularity in a vigorously acrimonious campaign. Her sense of justice and righteousness remained as strong as ever.

c h a p t e r   e l e v e n
"I'M GAME"

It came as no surprise that *Prayers for Bobby* came to Susan Sarandon's attention. The true story, about a gay youth who jumped off a bridge in 1983, largely because of the Christian-based homophobia of his mother, pushed all the right buttons in Sarandon. Sarandon immediately signed on to be executive producer and, in yet another bit of envelope pushing, intimated that she might be willing to play the mother.

Even more daring was the fact that *Prayers for Bobby* was being made for the normally very conservative CBS television network. "Considering the climate of this country, I was surprised when they said yes," Sarandon told the *Toronto Sun*. "I think it's very brave of them."

Unfortunately Sarandon ran afoul of creative differences with the producers. Earlier in her career, Sarandon would have gritted her teeth, as she did when filming *The Witches of Eastwick* and *Sweet Hearts Dance*, and hoped for the best. But there were some definite advantages to being who she was at the turn of the millennium and so she politely walked away from the project by saying, "I just felt the movie they wanted to make was not the movie I was interested in making."

What she was interested in early in 2001 was spending time with her family. With school back in session after the Christmas-New Year's break, Sarandon's Volvo, with the conspicuous "Kill Your Television" bumper sticker, was a regular presence on the car pool circuit . She could often be seen walking through the streets of New York City, dressed down to the point of unrecognizability. All of which is the way Sarandon liked to conduct her life.

These were interesting times on the family front. Eva had quickly made the transition from teenager to young woman and was slowly but surely venturing off on her own. Her sons had also gotten to an age when they were needing less and less of their mother's attention. Sarandon was admittedly torn.

"You want your kids to be safe and happy but you resist the temptation to let them go. You want to encourage them but eventually you have to love them enough not to control their lives."

With the new year, Sarandon was becoming increasingly aware of a looming screen actors and screen writers strike, once again centered on issues of money and, for the writers, the all-important screen credit. Not unexpectedly, Sarandon was in sympathy with both unions and was fully prepared to sit out what many were predicting would be a long and crippling strike.

But the pending strike was indirectly working to the

advantage of Sarandon as a number of projects of interest that had been bogged down in development were now suddenly being rushed into production in order to beat the almost certain strike deadline.

Sarandon became involved with several such projects-in-development early in 2001. The actress was in serious negotiations to star in the small independent film *Rialto*, a drama set against the 1950s Red Scare in which her character, who runs a small-town independent movie theater and has an affair with a young ex-POW, becomes the target of a Communist witch-hunt.

Sarandon was amused that at the center of *Rialto* was yet another older woman-younger man romance. "They keep paying me to jump into the sack with these guys," she told the *Guardian*. "There is no reason why a middle-aged woman shouldn't have the same needs as a middle-aged man. It's brave of some moviemakers to head in that direction. I'm game."

Of more immediate interest, with a protracted actors and writers strike looming on the horizon, was the dark comedy *Baby's in Black* in which a man falls in love with another woman while living with his dead girlfriend's parents. Sarandon, who would play the dead woman's mother, would reportedly make her biggest payday to date, an estimated $7 to $8 million.

Also green-lighted for 2001 was *The Banger Sisters* in which Sarandon and Goldie Hawn played two old friends and former rock-and-roll groupies who meet up years later and deal with their past. Sarandon, whose daughter, Eva, was considered for the part of Sarandon's daughter in the movie, played a socialite who is trying to put her past behind her. Also on the lighter side, Sarandon agreed to star in the comedy *Igby Goes Down*, opposite Claire Danes and Ryan Phillippe.

Also in development is a western called *Quietus* in which Sarandon would star (and produce) the coming-of-age story of a woman and her three sons. Sarandon is reportedly interested in doing the film with her *Anywhere But Here* director, Wayne Wang. Another project, *Denial*, would put Sarandon back in a political drama in which she plays a Jewish civil rights attorney who is brought into a controversial First Amendment case in which she must defend a colleague who denies that the Holocaust ever happened. Yet another true-life story, *A Class Divided*, would have Sarandon play a teacher who teaches a controversial class about racism.

During this period Sarandon also found the time to narrate a pair of documentaries on the human condition, *900 Women* and *Uphill All the Way*, as well as appearing in front of the camera for a documentary look at famous women celebrities called *Time of Our Lives*.

And, returning to voice-over work, Sarandon created the voice of a world-weary dog in a world of espionage between a group of dogs and cats in the film *Cats and Dogs*. The film was slated for a summer 2001 release. In January, Sarandon filmed a guest-starring role in the television situation comedy *Friends*, in which she did a hilarious self-mocking turn at the expense of her own image as a soap opera diva who becomes romantically involved with the younger character Joey. Moreover, the response to Sarandon's appearance in the previous season's episode of *Mad TV* was so positive that she willingly returned in the 2001 season for an episode in which she portrayed a tooth fairy with an attitude.

Although her choices entering the new year were conspicuous by their quirkiness, they were also marked by quality stories and solid filmmakers, and were, in essence, part and parcel of the slightly unorthodox choices she has been making all her life. Sarandon has often stated that, despite having two quite insightful and intelligent agents, the final choices remain hers and that she is not above having fun with or poking and prodding at the image she had spent so many years cultivating.

"If you get into that icon realm and you don't keep a sense of humor about yourself, it can be personally destructive to you and your craft," she once said. "I didn't want to get to the point where I couldn't poke fun at myself and have fun."

Fun was definitely her agenda midway through 2000 when she had agreed to narrate a children's record album entitled *Dinosongs: Poems to Celebrate a T-Rex Named Sue*. She was shocked to discover in January that what she had considered a minor diversion had made a fairly big splash and resulted in Sarandon receiving her first Grammy nomination for Best Spoken Word Album for Children.

For Sarandon and the rest of Ralph Nader's Green

Party supporters the New Year was also marked by the disappointment that their candidate did not capture the
White House. But the moral victory was just as sweet.
Nader had made a respectable showing in a number of
states and had sent a message to the political establishment that there was growing discontent abroad in the
political landscape that would have to be addressed.

But, in the inevitable finger-pointing coming in the
wake of the controversial ending to the election, Nader
and his supporters were clearly targeted as the cause for
Al Gore's narrow loss and the election of the much-
maligned George W. Bush.

For Sarandon, those kinds of charges were nothing
new and were the latest chapter in her odyssey of involvement that had often made her a target.

"I've been singled out, rewarded, or hated for my political activity, which has been going on for years. Once
you're identified as someone who cares, you're targeted by
both sides. Although it may not seem like it to some
people, I've been cautious in terms of following my heart
and making sure my head is clear."

Likewise, she is philosophical when looking back on her
career and the number of unorthodox but, in many cases,
successful choices she has made. "I've attracted watershed
films," she once said. "Movies that are very controversial.
They all hit very specific political and social changes that
I've gone through. I think you choose projects to come into
your life. And in doing so, in being true to yourself, it
reflects what's going on for yourself and a lot of people."

Consequently, it is not an unlikely scenario that Sarandon will shortly be off, exercising her freedoms in the name of political and social causes, and will continue to push the envelope of her still-emerging talents. She has given a new name to intelligence, sexuality, and blinding instinct as it plays out in her life and those around her. However long she chooses to play at life, in the end hers will be a proud legacy.

What has ultimately gotten Susan Sarandon this far, as a consummate actress and as a savvy person actively involved in the political landscape, is a fairly straightforward equation and one whose simplicity assures that whatever endeavor, be it personal or professional, that Sarandon pursues in the future will have meaning and resonance.

"To me, the challenge is to be incredibly good at your craft and, at the same time, to be connected to the world in some way. When you can contribute and pay your debt to that world, then you're really balancing a lot of things. To be completely self-indulgent and eccentric and become famous is not that difficult."

"Trying to deal with real life at the same time, that's when it gets tricky."

And at the end of the day she looks back on a life that has been described as "a melodrama with too many subplots" as her badge of honor.

"I could never have predicted the way my life has turned out. Any of it. My life is much more interesting than anything that I could have come up with."

FILMOGRAPHY

MOTION PICTURES

JOE
(1970)
Sarandon played the role of Melissa Compton.

THE APPRENTICE
(1971)
Sarandon played the role of Elizabeth Hawkins.

LADY LIBERTY
(1971)
Sarandon played the role of Sally.

LOVIN' MOLLY
(1974)
Sarandon played the role of Sarah.

SUSAN SARANDON

THE FRONT PAGE
(1974)
Sarandon played the role of Peggy Grant.

THE GREAT WALDO PEPPER
(1975)
Sarandon played the role of Mary Beth.

THE ROCKY HORROR PICTURE SHOW
(1975)
Sarandon played the role of Janet Weiss.

THE GREAT SMOKEY ROADBLOCK
(1976)
Sarandon played the role of Ginny.

DRAGONFLY
(1976)
Sarandon played the role of Chloe.

CHECKERED FLAG OR CRASH
(1977)
Sarandon played the role of C. C. Wainwright.

THE OTHER SIDE OF MIDNIGHT
(1977)
Sarandon played the role of Catherine Alexander Souglas.

PRETTY BABY
(1978)
Sarandon played the role of Hattie.

KING OF THE GYPSIES
(1978)
Sarandon played the role of Rose.

SOMETHING SHORT OF PARADISE
(1979)
Sarandon played the role of Madeline Ross.

ATLANTIC CITY
(1980)
Sarandon played the role of Sally.

LOVING COUPLES
(1980)
Sarandon played the role of Stephanie.

TEMPEST
(1982)
Sarandon played the role of Aretha.

THE HUNGER
(1983)
Sarandon played the role of Sarah Roberts.

SUSAN SARANDON

THE BUDDY SYSTEM
(1984)
Sarandon played the role of Emily.

COMPROMISING POSITIONS
(1985)
Sarandon played the role of Judith Singer.

THE WITCHES OF EASTWICK
(1987)
Sarandon played the role of Jane Spofford.

SWEET HEARTS DANCE
(1988)
Sarandon played the role of Sandra Boon.

BULL DURHAM
(1988)
Sarandon played the role of Annie Savoy.

THE JANUARY MAN
(1989)
Sarandon played the role of Christine Starkey.

A DRY WHITE SEASON
(1989)
Sarandon played the role of Melanie Bruwer.

WHITE PALACE
(1990)
Sarandon played the role of Nora Baker.

THELMA & LOUISE
(1991)
Sarandon played the role of Louise Sawyer.

LIGHT SLEEPER
(1991)
Sarandon played the role of Ann.

THE PLAYER
(1991)
Sarandon played the role of Susan Sarandon.

LORENZO'S OIL
(1992)
Sarandon played the role of Michaela Odone.

BOB ROBERTS
(1992)
Sarandon played the role of Tawna Titan.

LITTLE WOMEN
(1994)
Sarandon played the role of Marmee March.

SUSAN SARANDON

SAFE PASSAGE
(1994)
Sarandon played the role of Mag Singer.

THE CLIENT
(1994)
Sarandon played the role of Reggie Love.

DEAD MAN WALKING
(1995)
Sarandon played the character of Sister Helen Prejean.

JAMES AND THE GIANT PEACH
(1996)
Sarandon played the role of Spider.

TWILIGHT
(1998)
Sarandon played the role of Catherine Ames.

ILLUMINATA
(1998)
Sarandon played the role of Celimene.

STEPMOM
(1998)
Sarandon played the role of Jackie Harrison.

CRADLE WILL ROCK
(1999)
Sarandon played the role of Margherita Sarfetti.

ANYWHERE BUT HERE
(1999)
Sarandon played the role of Adele August.

OUR FRIEND MARTIN
(1999)
Sarandon played the role of Mrs. Clark.

JOE GOULD'S SECRET
(2000)
Sarandon played the role of Alice Neel.

RUGRATS IN PARIS: THE MOVIE
(2000)
Sarandon played the role of Coco La Bouche.

CATS AND DOGS
(2001)
Sarandon played the role of Ivy.

SUSAN SARANDON

TELEVISION MOVIES

F. SCOTT FITZGERALD AND THE LAST OF THE
    BELLES
(1974)
Sarandon played the role of Ailie Calhoun.

JUNE MOON
(1974)
Character name not available.

WHO AM I THIS TIME?
(1981)
Sarandon played the role of Helene Shaw.

A.D. ANNO DOMINI
(1985)
Sarandon played the role of Livilla.

MUSSOLINI: THE DECLINE AND FALL OF IL DUCE
(1985)
Sarandon played the role of Edda Ciano.

WOMEN OF VALOR
(1986)
Sarandon played the role of Colonel Margaret Ann
Jessup.

EARTHLY POSSESSIONS
(1999)
Sarandon played the role of Charlotte Emory.

TELEVISION SERIES

A WORLD APART
(1971–72)
Sarandon played the role of Patrice Kahlman.

SEARCH FOR TOMORROW
(1972)
Sarandon played the role of Sarah Fairbanks.

TELEVISION APPEARANCES

SESAME STREET
(1969)
Sarandon played the role of Susan.

OWEN MARSHALL: COUNSELOR AT LAW
(1971)
Sarandon played the role of Judy.

CARLUCCI'S DEPARTMENT
(1973)
Character name not available.

245

SUSAN SARANDON

INSIDE THE ACTORS STUDIO
(1994)
Sarandon was interviewed.

THE SIMPSONS
(1995)
Sarandon played the role of Bart's ballet teacher.

MAD TV
(2000)
Sarandon guest-starred as herself.

FRIENDS
(2001)
Sarandon played the role of Jessica Lockhart.

MAD TV
(2001)
Sarandon played the role of the Tooth Fairy.

PRODUCER CREDITS

THE GREAT SMOKEY ROADBLOCK
(1976)
Sarandon served as coproducer.

STEPMOM
(1998)
Sarandon served as executive producer.

THEATER CREDITS

AN EVENING WITH RICHARD NIXON AND . . .
(1972)

A COUPLA WHITE CHICKS SITTING AROUND
    TALKING
(1981)

EXTREMITIES
(1983)

DOCUMENTARIES

AIDS: THE FACTS OF LIFE
(1989)
Sarandon was interviewed.

THE CELLULOID CLOSET
(1995)
Sarandon was interviewed.

TELL THE TRUTH AND RUN: GEORGE SELDES
AND THE AMERICAN PRESS
(1996)
Sarandon served as narrator.

THE NEED TO KNOW
(1997)
Sarandon served as narrator.

FATHER ROY: INSIDE THE SCHOOL OF ASSASSINS
(1997)
Sarandon served as narrator.

187: DOCUMENTED
(1997)
Sarandon did voice-over work.

THE SECRET LIFE OF GEISHA
(1999)
Sarandon served as narrator.

THIS IS WHAT DEMOCRACY LOOKS LIKE
(2000)
Sarandon served as narrator.

TIME OF OUR LIVES
(2000)
Sarandon was an interviewee.

900 WOMEN
(2001)
Sarandon served as narrator.

UPHILL ALL THE WAY
(2001)
Sarandon served as narrator.

BIBLIOGRAPHY

BOOKS

Current Biography Yearbook 1998. New York: H. W. Wilson Co.

Sammon, Paul M. *Ridley Scott: Close Up.* New York: Thunder's Mouth Press, 1999.

INTERVIEW

Glasser, Ira. Interview by author. American Civil Liberties Union, New York, N.Y.

NEWSPAPER AND MAGAZINE ARTICLES

Abcarian, Robin. "Apple Pie, Motherhood and Sex." *Los Angeles Times*, 24 October 1999.

Altman, Sheryl. "Simply Unpredictable." *Women.com*, August 1999.

Arrington. Carl Wayne. "Lost in America." *Premiere*, April 1991.

Ball, Aimee Lee. "Sarandon, Seriously." *Mother Jones*, February–March 1989.

Black, Jonathan. "Susan Sarandon: 'It's Great Being a Sex Symbol.' " *Mademoiselle*, October 1982.

Blair, Ian. "Beam Her Up, Scotty, Susan Sarandon's Long Star Trek Finally May Be Reaching Fulfillment." *Chicago Tribune*, 12 June 1988.

Blau, Eleanor. "Susan Sarandon's Roughest Role." *New York Times*, 14 January 1983.

Blythe, Will. "The Siren." *Mirabella*, April 1999.

Bruni, Frank. "Susan Sarandon an Anomaly a Middle Aged Female Star." *Chicago Tribune*, 24 July 1994.

Cagle, Jess. "Laying Down the Law." *Entertainment Weekly*, 24 July 1994.

Carr, Jay. "Ms. Maverick." *Long Beach Press Telegram*, 25 May 1991.

———. "When Susan Sarandon Makes a Film, She Takes Her Politics with Her." *Boston Globe*, 30 May 1991.

Churchill, Bonnie. "Oscar Winner Breaks the Mold." *Christian Science Monitor*, 17 December 1999.

Cohen, Barney. "Susan Sarandon: No Longer the Ingenue!" *Cosmopolitan*, January 1984.

Collins, Gail. "Perfect Balance." *McCalls*, January 2000.

Dawes, Amy. "A Test of Their Relationship." *Sacramento Bee*, 14 January 1996.

Demaris, Ovid. "Most of All the Children Matter." *Parade*, 1 March 1992.

DiClementi, Deborah. "Queen of the Chick Flicks." *More*, November 1999.

Essex, Andrew. "Mothering Heights." *Entertainment Weekly*, 27 November 1998.

Flatley, Guy. "Susan Sarandon Summons Stardom." *Cosmopolitan*, March 1978.

Florence, Mari. "Star's Conscience Shines." *Variety*, 10 March 1998.

Fuller, Graham. "The Bigger Picture Revolution." *Interview*, October 1994.

Ganem, Mark. "Rockin' Robbins." *W*, December 1999.

Gerosa, Melina. "A Woman of Substance." *Ladies Home Journal*, November 1997.

Gerrard, Nicci. "A Voice for the Damned." *Out to Play*, 1996.

Gilbert, Matthew. "Sarandon Shows No Sign of Slowing Down." *Boston Globe*, 23 September 1992.

Givens, Ron. "The Twilight Hour." *New York Daily News*, 1998.

Goldman, Steve. "Careering Ahead." *London Sunday Times*, 15 March 1992.

Gray, Beverly. "Real Woman Walking." *Hollywood Reporter*, 12 March 1998.

Hamill, Dennis. "Not So Suddenly Susan." *New York Daily News*, 7 November 1999.

Hayward, Jeff. "Susan Sarandon Fits the Bill as Mother and Advocate On and Off the Screen." *Chicago Tribune*, 29 January 1995.

Hobson, Louis B. "Mother's Day." *Calgary Sun*, 7 November 1999.

Hobson, Louis B. "Reconcilable Differences." *Calgary Sun*, 14 January 1996.

———. "Robbins Puts Politics Aside." *Calgary Sun*, 14 January 1996.

———. "Sarandon Does Vegas." *Calgary Sun*, 31 October 2000.

Hofler, Robert, "The Anti Star." *Buzz*, February 1995.

Howard, David. "Llamas with Love." *People On Line*, 10 April 2000.

Hunter, Stephen. "Sarandon's Mother Lode of Talent." *Washington Post*, 20 December 1998.

Jacobs, Gloria. "Susan Sarandon." *Ms*, January–February 1996.

Jeffries, Daniel. "A Very Grown Up Kind of Glamour." *London Independent*, 24 March 1996.

Brian D. Johnson, "Reinventing Motherhood." *Macleans*, 8 November 1999.

Johnston, Sheila. "It's Just a Chance to Use My Celebrity." *London Independent*, 2 April 2000.

Kirkland, Bruce. "Sarandon Minus the Bull." *Toronto Sun*, 7 November 1999.

Laskas, Jeanne Marie. "Susan Sarandon: Rebel with 100 Causes." *Redbook*, April 1992.

Laugley, Leonora. "Savvy Susan." *Elle*, October 1990.

MacMinn, Aleene. "Sarandon Rips Press." *Los Angeles Times*, 28 May 1991.

Mancini, Joseph. "The Other Side of Sarandon." *Attentzione*, July 1980.

Mann, Roderick. "Sarandon on a Role of Sorts." *Los Angeles Times*, 2 September 1982.

Mansfield, Stephanie. "A Dangerous Man." *GQ*, October 1992.

Maude, Colette. "Shoot from the Hip." *Time Out*, March 1992.

Mcalevey, Peter. "The Mother of Us All." *Venice*, December 1995.

McBride, Murdoch. "Susan Sarandon Steps Up to Face City Hall." *Backstage*, 14 May 1999.

McLeod, Tyler. "Super Susan." *Calgary Sun*, 16 December 1998.

———. "Christmas Presence." *Calgary Sun*, 12 December 1998.

Mills, Nancy. "An Outta the Ballpark Look at Baseball." *Los Angeles Times*, 21 June 1988.

Mottram, James. "Whatever Happened to Wayne Wang?" *Empire* 1998.

Newman, Bruce. "Susan Sarandon: Lover, Lawyer, Marmee." *New York Times*, 17 July 1994.

Orton, Chip. "Hollywood's Bad Girl Is a Homebody at Heart." *US*, 23 January 1979.

Pacheco, Patrick. "Pretty Mama." *After Dark*, June 1978.

Palmer, Martyn. "Tim Robbins: Why I'll Always Be a Misfit." *Herald Sun*, 30 April 2000.

Plutzik, Roberta. "Susan Sarandon." *Moviegoer*, October 1982.

Queenan, Joe. "Miss Congeniality." *Rolling Stone*, 9 February 1989.

Randle, Nancy Jalasca. "Rolling with Her Changes, Susan Sarandon Continues to Ripen with Age." *Chicago Tribune*, 14 March 1999.

Rauzi, Robin. "Oscar Officials Slam Presenters' Political Plugs." *Los Angeles Times*, 31 March 1993.

Reilley, Beatrice. "Sarandon Speaks in Ackerman." *UCLA Daily Bruin*, 18 January 1984.

Robbins, Tim, and Susan Sarandon. "Our 23 Seconds at the Oscar." *Los Angeles Times*, April 1993.

Ryan, James. "Sarandon Takes Her Vows for Walking." *Long Beach Press Telegram*, 4 January 1996.

Sarandon, Susan. Interview by Claudia Dreifus. *Progressive*, October 1989.

———. Interview by Claudia Dreifus. *Playboy*, May 1989.

———. Interview by Marshall Fine. *Playboy*, February 1995.

———. Interview by James Kaplan. *US*, February 2000.

———. "Stepmom: Interview with Susan Sarandon." By Prairie Miller. *Bigstar*, 1999.

———.Interview by Adrian Wootton. *Guardian*, 12 November 1999.

Scheer, Robert. "Unmarried with Children and Values." *Los Angeles Times*, 30 August 1992.

Scheinbart, Betsy. "Sarandon Lends a Hand to Hungry." *New York Daily News*, 19 November 1999.

Seymour, Gene. "She's Her Own Best Counsel." *Los Angeles Times*, 17 July 1994.

Smith, Greg B. "Rudy Blasted at Rally." *New York Daily News*, 2 October 1999.

Stevenson, Jane. "Sarandon Makes Her Own Role." *Toronto Sun*, 30 December 1998.

Taylor, Clarke. "Beyond Witchcraft, Susan Sarandon

Doesn't Like All She Sees." *Chicago Tribune*, 14 June 1987.

Wadler, Joyce. "Rough Edges and Lingerie." *Rolling Stone,* 28 May 1981.

Walsh, Rebecca Ascher. "Labor of Love: With Dead Man Walking, Susan Sarandon and Tim Robbins Go from Oscar Outlaws to Golden Couple." *Entertainment Weekly*, 22 March 1996.

Werner, Laurie. "Susan Sarandon." *Ambience*, August 1978.

Yagoda, Ben. "The Prime of Susan Sarandon." *American Film*, May 1991.

WEB SITES

Bigstar.com

Google Search

Hollywood Academy

Internet Movie Data Base

Jam Showbiz

Mr. Showbiz

New York Daily News Online

People On Line

Susan Sarandon Site

Tim Robbins Page

UVA Newsmakers

Women.com

CHAPTER NOTES

**CHAPTER ONE: "WE ARE PISSED OFF!
HAPPY MOTHER'S DAY!"**

p. 15 "We are pissed . . .": *New York Daily News Online*, 18 April 2000.

p. 16 "I told time that . . .": *Calgary Sun*, January 2000.

p. 19 "Laura Schlessinger is . . .": Sheila Johnston, "It's Just a Chance to Use My Celebrity," *London Independent*, 2 April 2000.

p. 22 "By doing so I . . .": Marti Florence, "Star's Conscience Shines," *Variety*, 10 March 1998.

p. 23 "There's nothing dilletantish . . .": Bruce Newman, "Susan Sarandon: Lover, Lawyer, Marmee," *New York Times*, 17 July 1994.

p. 23 "She's my role model . . .": Jeanne Marie Laskas, "Susan Sarandon: Rebel with 100 Causes," *Redbook*, April 1992.

p. 23 "She understands her place . . .": Robin

Abcarian, "Apple Pie, Motherhood and Sex," *Los Angeles Times*, 24 October 1999.

p. 23 "You don't feel jealous . . .": Robin Abcarian, "Apple Pie, Motherhood and Sex," *Los Angeles Times*, 24 October 1999.

p. 24 "Whenever you're trying . . .": Beverly Gray, "Real Woman Walking," *Hollywood Reporter*, 12 March 1998.

p. 26 "She is regarded by . . .": Joseph Mancini, "The Other Side of Sarandon," *Attentzione*, July 1980.

p. 26 "She is a big star . . .": Bruce Newman, "Susan Sarandon: Lover, Lawyer, Marmee," *New York Times*, 17 July 1994.

p. 26 "But she's a great . . .": Martyn Palmer, "Tim Robbins: Why I'll Always Be a Misfit," *Herald Sun*, 30 April 2000.

p. 27 "I believe in love . . .": Guy Flatley, "Susan Sarandon Summons Stardom," *Cosmopolitan*, March 1978.

p. 27 "I'm always incredibly . . .": Sheila Johnston, "It's Just a Chance to Use My Celebrity," *London Independent*, 2 April 2000.

CHAPTER TWO: "I WAS A SPACEY CHILD"

p. 29 "I was a spacey . . .": Joyce Wadler, "Rough Edges and Lingerie," *Rolling Stone*, 28 May 1981.

p. 29 "both had very strange . . .": Joyce Wadler, "Rough Edges and Lingerie," *Rolling Stone*, 28 May 1981.

p. 33 "I was a very spacey . . .": Laurie Werner, "Susan Sarandon," *Ambience*, August 1978.

p. 34 "It grounded me . . .": Chip Orton, "Hollywood's Bad Girl Is a Homebody at Heart," *US*, 23 January 1979.

p. 35 "It wasn't a house . . .": Aimee Lee Ball, "Sarandon, Seriously," *Mother Jones*, February–March 1989.

p. 35 "I was asking all . . .": Robert Hofler, "The Anti-Star," *Buzz*, February 1995.

p. 37 "It was a great . . .": Joyce Wadler, "Rough Edges and Lingerie," *Rolling Stone*, 28 May 1981.

p. 39 "My parents had no chance . . .": Deborah DiClementi, "Queen of the Chick Flicks," *More*, November 1999.

p. 39 "There is absolutely no . . .": Jeanne Marie Laskas, "Susan Sarandon: Rebel with 100 Causes," *Redbook*, April 1992.

p. 39 "Which may have something . . .": *Hollywood Reporter*, August 1988.

p. 40 "because that's what you did . . .": *Current Biography Yearbook 1998* (New York: H. W. Wilson Co.).

p. 40 "My sole ambition was . . .": Leonora Laugley, "Savvy Susan," *Elle*, October 1990.

p. 41 "I never studied . . .": *Parade*, 21 June 1981.

p. 42 "I did some modeling . . .": Interview by Claudia Dreifus, *Playboy*, May 1989.

p. 44 "When you're that age . . .": Will Blythe, "The Siren," *Mirabella*, April 1999.

p. 45 "The point of being twenty . . .": Graham Fuller,

"The Bigger Picture Revolution," *Interview,* October 1994.

p. 46 "We decided it would . . .": Joyce Wadler, "Rough Edges and Lingerie," *Rolling Stone*, 28 May 1981.

p. 46 "My marriage got me . . .": Will Blythe, "The Siren," *Mirabella*, April 1999.

p. 48 "he would have a . . .": *Parade*, 21 June 1981.

p. 49 "They asked me to do . . .": Ben Yagoda, "The Prime of Susan Sarandon," *American Film*, May 1991.

p. 49 "I remember calling . . .": Patrick Pacheco, "Pretty Mama," *After Dark*, June 1978.

CHAPTER THREE: "I DON'T KNOW IF PEOPLE CONSIDER ME A PAIN IN THE ASS"

p. 51 "I don't know if . . .": Aimee Lee Ball, "Sarandon, Seriously," *Mother Jones*, February–March 1989.

p. 52 "I remember asking him . . .": "Pretty Mama," *After Dark*, Patrick Pacheco, June 1978.

p. 52 "I never knew . . .": Interview by Claudia Dreifus, *Playboy*, May 1989.

p. 53 "All I know was . . .": Peter Mcalevey, "The Mother of Us All," *Venice*, December 1995.

p. 54 "I didn't even consider . . .": Jay Carr, "When Susan Sarandon Makes a Film, She Takes Her Politics with Her," *Boston Globe*, 30 May 1991.

p. 57 "Our reasons for . . .": Chip Orton, "Hollywood's Bad Girl Is a Homebody at Heart," *US*, 23 January 1979.

p. 57 "We are growing apart . . .": Leonora Laughley, "Savvy Susan," *Elle,* October 1990.

p. 58 "I thought he was . . .": Aimee Lee Ball, "Sarandon, Seriously," *Mother Jones*, February–March 1989.

p. 62 "When the producers asked . . .": Eleanor Blau, "Susan Sarandon's Roughest Role," *New York Times*, 14 January 1983.

p. 65 "The news reporters don't . . .": Interview by Claudia Dreifus, *Progressive*, October 1989.

p. 67 "I just knew more . . .": Roberta Plutzik, "Susan Sarandon," *Moviegoer*, October 1982.

p. 68 "It was never meant . . .": Roberta Plutzik, "Susan Sarandon," *Moviegoer*, October 1982.

p. 69 "I don't know if . . .": Aimee Lee Ball, "Sarandon, Seriously," *Mother Jones*, February–March 1989.

p. 71 "When I turned down . . .": Patrick Pacheco, "Pretty Mama," *After Dark*, June 1978.

p. 71 "Suddenly I was asked . . .": Guy Flatley, "Susan Sarandon Summons Stardom," *Cosmopolitan*, March 1978.

p. 73 "It is difficult . . .": Guy Flatley, "Susan Sarandon Summons Stardom," *Cosmopolitan*, March 1978.

p. 76 "I work best in . . .": Stephen Hunter, "Sarandon's Mother Load of Talent," *Washington Post*, 20 December 1998.

p. 77 "My mother thinks . . .": Chip Orton, "Hollywood's Bad Girl Is a Homebody at Heart," *US*, 23 January 1979.

p. 77 "He (Chris) was . . .": Interview by Claudia Dreifus, *Playboy,* May 1989.

p. 77 "I no longer . . .": Barney Cohen, "Susan Sarandon: No Longer the Ingenue!" *Cosmopolitan*, January 1984.

CHAPTER FOUR: "SO I DECIDED TO LEARN ABOUT NICARAGUA"

p. 79 "So I decided to . . .": Susan Bolotin, "Taking Diplomacy into Their Own Hands," *Vogue*, July 1984.

p. 79 "I've pretty much accepted . . .": Jonathan Black, "Susan Sarandon: "It's Great Being a Sex Symbol," *Mademoiselle*, October 1982.

p. 87 "I deal with reality . . .": Guy Flatley, "Susan Sarandon Summons Stardom," *Cosmopolitan*, March 1978.

p. 88 "You try and talk . . .": Joyce Wadler, "Rough Edges and Lingerie," *Rolling Stone*, 28 May 1981.

p. 90 "I thought, "What a . . .": Interview by Claudia Dreifus, *Playboy*, May 1989.

p. 91 "I didn't know it . . .": Barney Cohen, "Susan Sarandon: No Longer the Ingenue!" *Cosmopolitan*, January 1984.

p. 93 "After he died . . .": Claudia Dreifus, "Susan Sarandon," *Progressive*, October 1989.

p. 94 "I didn't know her . . .": *Current Biography Yearbook 1989* (New York: H. W. Wilson Co.).

p. 95 "I just got sick . . .": Ben Yagoda, "The Prime of Susan Sarandon," *American Film*, May 1991.

p. 96 "I wound up playing . . .": Roberta Plutzik, "Susan Sarandon," *Moviegoer*, October 1982.

p. 97 "I had so many . . .": Melina Gerosa, "A Woman of Substance," *Ladies Home Journal*, November 1997.

p. 98 "But I was completely . . .": Robert Scheer, "Unmarried with Children and Values," *Los Angeles Times*, 30 August 1992.

p. 99 "I've always had . . .": Interview by Claudia Dreifus, *Playboy*, May 1989.

p. 100 "I definitely was . . .": *Lesbian News*, 1999 (Susan Sarandon Site).

p. 101 "Every traumatic . . .": Jonathan Black, "Susan Sarandon: 'It's Great Being a Sex Symbol,' " *Mademoiselle*, October 1982.

p. 102 "I have two brothers . . .": Susan Bolotin, "Taking Diplomacy into Their Own Hands," *Vogue*, July 1984.

p. 105 "I tried to talk . . .": Interview by Claudia Dreifus, *Playboy*, May 1989.

p. 105 "At one point you . . .": Beatrice Reilley, "Sarandon Speaks at Ackerman," *UCLA Daily Bruin*, 18 January 1984.

p. 105 "I decided to make the . . .": Interview by Claudia Dreifus, *Playboy*, May 1989.

p. 108 "I suppose they did not . . .": Colette Maude, "Shooting from the Hip," *Time Out,* 11–18 March 1992.

p. 110 "One of the things . . .": Interview with Ira Glasser, January 2001.

p. 110 "I would have been . . .": Interview with Ira Glasser, January 2001.

p. 111 "It was total serious . . .": Interview with Ira Glasser, January 2001.

p. 112 "The whole issue was contained . . .": Interview with Ira Glasser, January 2001.

p. 112 "This isn't about . . .": Barney Cohen, "Susan Sarandon: No Longer the Ingenue!" *Cosmopolitan*, January 1984.

p. 114 "After I contracted . . .": Melina Gerosa, "A Woman of Substance," *Ladies Home Journal,* November 1997.

p. 114 "It was pretty loose . . .": Interview by Claudia Dreifus, *Playboy*, May 1989.

p. 115 "The baby was probably . . .": Aimee Lee Ball, "Sarandon, Seriously," *Mother Jones*, February–March 1989.

p. 115 "If my daughter hadn't . . .": Nancy Mills, "An Outta the Ballpark Look at Baseball," *Los Angeles Times*, 21 June 1988.

p. 116 "It paid for my . . .": Ben Yagoda, "The Prime of Susan Sarandon," *American Film*, May 1991.

CHAPTER FIVE: "THE LONELINESS OF THAT PERIOD WAS HORRIBLE"

p. 117 "The loneliness of that period . . .": Dennis Hamill, "Not So Suddenly Susan," *New York Daily News*, 7 November 1999.

p. 119 "I was feeling particularly . . .": Aimee Lee Ball,

"Sarandon, Seriously," *Mother Jones*, February–March 1989.

p. 122 "The loneliness of that period . . .": Dennis Hamill, "Not So Suddenly Susan," *New York Daily News*, 7 November 1999.

p. 124 "Since there was no through . . .": Gavin Smith, "Uncompromising Positions," *Film Comment*, March–April 1993.

p. 124 "I learned that a promise . . .": Clarke Taylor, "Beyond Witchcraft, Susan Sarandon Doesn't Like All She Sees," *Chicago Tribune*, 14 June 1987.

p. 125 "I think they . . .": Clarke Taylor, "Beyond Witchcraft, Susan Sarandon Doesn't Like All She Sees," *Chicago Tribune*, 14 June 1987.

p. 126 "Not only was I not . . .": Ben Yagoda, "The Prime of Susan Sarandon," *American Film*, May 1991.

p. 126 "I was always called in . . .": "Sarandon Shows No Sign of Slowing Down," Matthew Gilbert, *Boston Globe*, 23 September 1992.

p. 129 "Annie could have easily . . .": Ben Yagoda, "The Prime of Susan Sarandon," *American Film*, May 1991.

p. 130 "My daughter chose him . . .": Melina Gerosa, "A Woman of Substance," *Ladies Home Journal*, November 1997.

p. 131 "When a person sees . . .": "It Comes Down to Really Seeing Others, Sensitive and Sexy Sarandon Says," *Milwaukee Journal Sentinal*, 25 December 1998.

p. 131 "He seemed like a . . .": Stephanie Mansfield, "A Dangerous Man," *GQ*, October 1992.

p. 132 "It's not like we're . . .": Interview by James Kaplan, *US*, 2000.

p. 137 "Two misfits taking . . .": Matthew Gilbert, "Sarandon Shows No Sign of Slowing Down," *Boston Globe*, 23 September 1992.

p. 138 "It's frustrating . . .": Ben Yagoda, "The Prime of Susan Sarandon," *American Film*, May 1991.

p. 140 "I wasn't operating . . .": Aimee Lee Ball, "Sarandon, Seriously," *American Film*, February–March 1989.

p. 141 "I felt it was an . . .": Claudia Dreifus, "Susan Sarandon," *Progressive*, October 1989.

p. 143 "You've got a lot of . . .": Ben Yagoda, "The Prime of Susan Sarandon," *American Film*, May 1991.

p. 143 "Thanks, I hope . . .": Ben Yagoda, "The Prime of Susan Sarandon," *American Film*, May 1991.

CHAPTER SIX: "IT WAS A VERY SCARY TIME"

p. 145 "It was a very . . .": Robert Scheer, "Unmarried with Children and Values," *Los Angeles Times*, 30 August 1992.

p. 147 "Nowadays I think I . . .": Ron Givens, "The Twilight Hour," *New York Daily News*, 3 March 1998.

p. 147 "What I want for . . .": Jeff Hayward, "Susan Sarandon Fits the Bill as Mother and Advocate On and Off the Screen," *Chicago Tribune*, 29 January 1995.

p. 148 "I think that Clinton is . . .": Robert Scheer,

"Unmarried with Children and Values," *Los Angeles Times*, 30 August 1992.

p. 150 "The message was clear . . .": Robert Hofler, "The Anti Star," *Buzz*, February 1995.

p. 150 "It was a scary . . .": Robert Scheer, "Unmarried with Children and Values," *Los Angeles Times*, 30 August 1992.

p. 152 "She's always inventive . . .": Paul M. Sammon, *Ridley Scott: Up Close* (New York: Thunder's Mouth Press, 1999).

p. 152 "The first thing I . . .": Daniel Jeffries, "A Very Grown Up Kind of Glamour," *London Independent*, 24 March 1996.

p. 152 "It's kind of like joining . . .": Carl Wayne Arrington, "Lost in America," *Premiere*, April 1991.

p. 153 "For a while we never . . .": Carl Wayne Arrington, "Lost in America," *Premiere*, April 1991.

p. 154 "I thought this was . . .": *Inside the Actors Studio* Interview.

p. 154 "The thing that worked . . .": Robert Scheer, "Unmarried with Children and Values," *Los Angeles Times*, 30 August 1992.

p. 154 "In that movie . . .": Stephen Hunter, "Sarandon's Mother Lode of Talent," *Washington Post*, 20 December 1998.

p. 157 "I'm the one who says . . .": Martyn Palmer, "Tim Robbins: Why I'll Always Be a Misfit," *Herald Sun*, 30 April 2000.

p. 157 "Recently somebody called . . .": Interview by Claudia Dreifus, *Playboy,* May 1989.

p. 159 "The Persian Gulf War . . .": Aleene MacMinn, "Sarandon Rips Press," *Los Angeles Times*, 28 May 1991.

p. 159 "I don't think we . . .": Robert Scheer, "Unmarried with Children and Values," *Los Angeles Times*, 30 August 1992.

p. 161 "It's quite liberating to pay . . .": Colette Maude, "Shoot from the Hip," *Time Out,* 11–18 March 1992.

p. 161 "But I liked the script and . . .": Dennis Hamill, "Not So Suddenly Susan," *New York Daily News*, 7 November 1999.

p. 162 "I just felt what happened . . .": Gavin Smith, "Uncompromising Positions," *Film Comment*, March–April 1993.

p. 164 "It's not exactly what . . .": Jess Cagle, "Laying Down the Law," *Entertainment Weekly*, 24 July 1994.

p. 165 "I guess this means . . .": Jay Carr, "When Susan Sarandon Makes a Film, She Takes Her Politcs With Her," *Boston Globe*, 30 May 1991.

p. 167 "I've never been so . . .": Robert Hofler, "The Anti Star," *Buzz,* February 1995.

p. 168 "Hearing people shouting . . .": Dennis Hamill, "Not So Suddenly Susan," *New York Daily News,* 7 November 1999.

p. 168 "It's not supposed to be . . .": Robin Rauzi, "Oscar Officials Slam Presenter's Political Plugs," *Los Angeles Times*, 31 March 1993.

p. 168 "For someone who I . . .": Robin Rauzi, "Oscar Officials Slam Presenter's Political Plugs," *Los Angeles Times*, 31 March 1993.

p. 169 "Was what we did . . .": Tim Robbins and Susan Sarandon, "Our 23 Seconds at the Oscars," *Los Angeles Times*, 2 April 1993.

p. 169 "Basically what Susan and . . .": Interview with Ira Glasser, January 2001.

CHAPTER SEVEN: "I ALREADY KNOW WHAT I THINK"

p. 171 "I already know . . .": Robin Abcarian, "Apple Pie, Motherhood and Sex," *Los Angeles Times*, 24 October 1999.

p. 171 "Some of them were . . .": Jess Cagle, "Laying Down the Law," *Entertainment Weekly*, 24 July 1994.

p. 172 "If I were 22 and . . .": Rebecca Ascher Walsh, "Labor of Love: With *Dead Man Walking*, Susan Sarandon and Tim Robbins Go from Oscar Outlaws to Golden Couple," *Entertainment Weekly*, 22 March 1996.

p. 173 "They always find a . . .": Rebecca Ascher Walsh, "Labor of Love: With *Dead Man Walking*, Susan Sarandon and Tim Robbins Go from Oscar Outlaws to Golden Couple," *Entertainment Weekly*, 22 March 1996.

p. 177 "My kids are so . . .": Gene Seymour, "She's Her Own Best Counsel," *Los Angeles Times*, 17 July 1994.

p. 178 "One afternoon . . .": *UVA Newsmakers*, 27 January 2000.

p. 179 "I kept saying to . . .": *UVA Newsmakers*, 27 January 2000.

p. 180 "I wanted to, had to . . .": Nicci Gerrard, "A Voice for the Damned," *Out to Play* (Google Search-Out to Play Web Site 1996).

p. 180 "Susan was the . . .": Louis B. Hobson, "Reconcilable Differences," *Calgary Sun,* 14 January 1996.

p. 181 "We told each other . . .": *Los Angeles Magazine*, June 97.

p. 182 "I almost dropped out . . .": Melina Gerosa, "A Woman of Substance," *Ladies Home Journal,* November 1997.

p. 184 "I've gone all the way . . .": James Ryan, "Sarandon Takes Her Vows for Walking," *Long Beach Press Telegram,* 4 January 1996.

p. 184 "We're not stupid . . .": Rebecca Ascher Walsh, "Labor of Love: With *Dead Man Walking*, Susan Sarandon and Tim Robbins Go from Oscar Outlaws to Golden Couple," *Entertainment Weekly*, 22 March 1996.

p. 184 "It was a nightmare . . .": Rebecca Ascher Walsh, "Labor of Love: With *Dead Man Walking*, Susan Sarandon and Tim Robbins Go from Oscar Outlaws to Golden Couple," *Entertainment Weekly*, 22 March 1996.

p. 185 "On this, it . . .": Rebecca Ascher Walsh, "Labor of Love: With *Dead Man Walking*, Susan Sarandon and Tim Robbins Go from Oscar Outlaws to Golden Couple," *Entertainment Weekly*, 22 March 1996.

p. 185 "We had four to six . . .": Robin Abcarian, "Apple Pie, Motherhood and Sex," *Los Angeles Times*, 24 October 1999.

p. 186 "I'm not gonna talk . . .": Robin Abcarian,

"Apple Pie, Motherhood and Sex," *Los Angeles Times*, 24 October 1999.

p. 187 "Susan deserves the . . .": Louis B. Hobson, "Reconcilable Differences," *Calgary Sun*, 14 January 1996.

p. 187 "I'm very good at . . .": Rebecca Ascher Walsh, "Labor of Love: With *Dead Man Walking*, Susan Sarandon and Tim Robbins Go from Oscar Outlaws to Golden Couple," *Entertainment Weekly*, 22 March 1996.

CHAPTER EIGHT: "I'M A DESIGNATED HITTER FOR OLDER OVARIES"

p. 189 "I'm a designated . . .": Robin Abcarian, "Apple Pie, Motherhood and Sex," *Los Angeles Times*, 24 October 1999.

p. 190 "I can't figure out what . . .": "It Comes Down to Really Seeing Others, Sensitive and Sexy Sarandon Says," *Milwaukee Journal Sentinel,* 25 December 1998.

p. 193 "She's always there . . .": Mari Florence, "Star's Conscience Shines," *Variety*, 10 March 1998.

p. 194 "I think everyone is . . .": Jeff Hayward, "Susan Sarandon Fits the Bill as Mother and Advocate On and Off the Screen," *Chicago Tribune*, 29 January 1995.

p. 195 "I think life is so . . .": Gene Seymour, "She's Her Own Best Counsel," *Los Angeles Times*, 17 July 1994.

p. 197 "I don't mind getting older . . .": Nicci Gerrard, "A Voice for the Damned," *Out to Play*, 1996.

p. 198 "I see how my life . . .": Mari Florence, "Star's Conscience Shines," *Variety*, 10 March 1998

CHAPTER NINE: "AM I GOING TO SHUT UP? NO"

p. 199 "Am I going to . . .": Jay Carr, "When Susan Sarandon Makes a Film, She Takes Her Politics with Her," *Boston Globe*, 30 May 1991.

p. 201 "If you make a movie . . .": Andrew Essex, "Mothering Heights," *Entertainment Weekly*, 27 November 1998.

p. 202 "We really worked . . .": "*Calgary Sun*, 20 December 1998.

p. 202 "You have to strip . . .": Andrew Essex, "Mothering Heights," *Entertainment Weekly*, 27 November 1998.

p. 203 "I just followed Susan . . .": Nancy Jalasca Randle, "Rolling with Her Changes, Susan Sarandon Continues to Ripen with Age," *Chicago Tribune*, 14 March 1999.

p. 204 "If we're not here . . .": Susan Sarandon Web Site News Archive.

p. 205 "As a woman, you hardly . . .": "*People On Line* Web Site 1999.

p. 206 "I thought she had a lot . . .": James Mottram, "Whatever Happened to Wayne Wang?" *Empire,* 1998.

p. 208 "No one's tapped into . . .": Brian D. Johnson, "Reinventing Motherhood," *Macleans*, 8 November 1999.

p. 208 "Lets get real . . .": Stephen Hunter, "Sarandon's Mother Lode of Talent," *Washington Post*, 20 December 1998.

p. 209 "I was terrified in the . . .": *People On Line* Web Site 1999.

p. 210 "I find it shocking . . .": Greg B. Smith, "Rudy Blasted at Rally," *New York Daily News*, 2 October 1999.

p. 211 "I thought it was pretty boring . . .": Louis B. Hobson, "Mother's Day," *Calgary Sun*, 7 November 1999.

p. 212 "I have it all . . .": Louis B. Hobson, "Mother's Day," *Calgary Sun*, 7 November 1999.

p. 212 "The Democratic Party . . .": Susan Sarandon Web Site News Archive.

CHAPTER TEN: "ANYBODY WHO VOTES SHOULD VOTE WITH THEIR HEART"

p. 215 "Anybody who votes . . .": Susan Sarandon Web Site News Archive.

p. 216 "I'm just so tired of . . .": Susan Sarandon Web Site News Archive.

p. 217 "I think when you've . . .": Susan Sarandon Web Site News Archive.

p. 218 "After about five hours . . .": Susan Sarandon Web Site News Archive.

p. 220 "My intent is to speak . . .": Susan Sarandon Web Site News Archive.

p. 220 "Plan to be surprised . . .": Susan Sarandon Web Site News Archive.

p. 221 "Dr. Laura has a . . .": Susan Sarandon Web Site News Archive.

p. 222 "You do what you can . . .": Murdoch McBride, "Susan Sarandon Steps Up to Face City Hall," *Backstage*, 14 May 1999.

p. 222 "I don't do as much as . . .": David Howard, "Llamas with Love," *People On Line*, 10 April 2000.

p. 223 "We stand a chance of . . .": Susan Sarandon Web Site News Archive.

p. 224 "These women can't . . .": Susan Sarandon Web Site News Archive.

p. 224 "There isn't enough dialogue . . .": Susan Sarandon Web Site News Archive.

p. 225 "I'm not all that worried . . .": Susan Sarandon Web Site News Archive.

p. 226 "People unfortunately . . .": Susan Sarandon Web Site News Archive.

p. 226 "It's a very . . .": Susan Sarandon Web Site News Archive.

p. 227 "I'm happy to finally be . . .": Susan Sarandon Web Site News Archive.

CHAPTER ELEVEN: "I'M GAME"

p. 229 "I'm game . . .": Andrew Wootton, "Susan Sarandon Interview," *Guardian*, 12 November 1999.

p. 233 "If you get into that . . .": Susan Sarandon Web Site News Archive.

p. 234 "I've been singled out . . .": Graham Fuller, "The Bigger Picture Revolution," *Interview*, October 1994.

p. 234 "I've attracted watershed . . .": Nancy Jalasca Randle, "Rolling with Her Changes, Susan Sarandon Continues to Ripen With Age," *Chicago Tribune*, 14 March 1999.

p. 235 "To me the challenge is . . .": Jonathan Black, "Susan Sarandon: It's Great Being a Sex Symbol," *Mademoiselle*, October 1982.

p. 235 "Trying to deal with . . .": Jeanne Marie Laskas, "Susan Sarandon: Rebel with 100 Causes," *Redbook*, April 1992.

p. 235 "as a melodrama with . . .": Jeanne Marie Laskas, "Susan Sarandon: Rebel with 100 Causes," *Redbook*, April 1992.

p. 235 "I could never have . . .": Jeanne Marie Laskas, "Susan Sarandon: Rebel with 100 Causes," *Redbook*, April 1992.

INDEX